ALCOHOL IN SOCIETY

PATTERNS AND ATTITUDES

KNUD-ERIK SABROE

Institute of Psychology, Aarhus University

Distributed by Aarhus University Press

PREFACE

A number of foundations and persons have made the production of this book possible. The articles represent part of a research activity which has been supported by the *Danish State Life Insurance Company, the State Research Councils, the Health Insurance Foundation, the Health Development Foundation, Aarhus University Research Foundation, the Tuborg Foundation and the Amsterdam Group*. In preparing the articles valuable comments have been received from *Karen Elmeland, Peter Nygaard, Ove Rasmussen, Peter Schiøler, Palle Schriver* and *Bo Sommerlund*. *Bjørn Stensvold* and *Birthe Henriksen* has typed the manuscripts. *Annie Dolmer Kristensen* has prepared the manuscripts for this book. Hardy Solskov has made the working drawing of the cover. To all my sincere thanks.

Knud-Erik Sabroe, June 1994

CONTENTS

INTRODUCTION

INTRODUCTION

In the spring of 1989, a major survey, comprising a representative population of 2,000 Danes above the age of fifteen and including 100 questions, was carried out. The survey was the first major data collection in the project the *Danes' Alcohol Consumer Consciousness*. Previously to this, a series of pilot investigations had been undertaken mainly using a qualitative interview method. Parallel to the quantitative methods, qualitative research has also been carried out, dealing with "Therapist consciousness" (cf. article 8), "Life history of heavy consumers" (Elmeland, Nygaard & Sabroe, 1990), and "The function of a treatment/prevention system" (Sabroe, 1993), the two latter published in Danish. The overall survey results will be documented in a major publication (planned for summer 1994), but some preliminary analysis, special topic reports and theoretical considerations have already been accomplished and presented to interest groups and at international research seminars or guest lectures.

In most cases these preliminary analyses have been turned into reports and they are often written in English. Three articles: 2, 6, and 7 have been translated into and published in Hungarian. Of the articles in this volume, numbers 1, 5, 6, 7 and 8 have been produced primarily for the purpose of presenting the results of Danish social science alcohol research in international connections. The case being that until recent years there has been little social science oriented alcohol research, the need to present data from the new and growing research has been pressing, therefore. This is due to the fact, also, that an increased concern with alcohol related problems - stimulated not least by the WHO "Health for all year 2000"-programme - and consequently with alcohol research, has been growing in Europe. In this connection the articles have been used as a basis for discussion in seminars in Belgium, Greece, Finland, Hungary, Iceland, Portugal, San Marino and Scotland. As the articles are analyses in their own right it has been found relevant to compile them in a publication representing project activities. As the reports have been produced as individual papers, they do *not* constitute a consecutive and strictly coherent picture. But the reports represent different aspects of the project course, being partly theoretical considerations, partly qualitative efforts and partly analyses of survey data; they all have their origin in the frame of understanding established around the concept of *Alcohol Consumer Consciousness.*

1. **Alcohol Consumer Consciousness. A social psychological perspective on alcohol.** This article is a first attempt at outlining the frame of understanding for the project. The core concept is Alcohol Consumer Consciousness, a concept embedded in social psychological thinking. The theoretical foundation is not based on any seperate theory, but besides general social psychology major inspiration has been provided by a phenomenologically-oriented psychology, culture-historic psychology and cognitive psychology. These orientations have played a role more as guiding principles or work hypotheses than as established paradigms for creation of concepts and methodology or for understanding. The article was originally written as background material for a workshop at the *35th International Congress on Alcoholism and Drug Dependence,* 1988, and was published in the proceedings from the conference (Sabroe, 1989).

2. **Alcohol consumption and the groups of society** is an (extended) English version of a chapter in Petersen et al. (1989). A research group, headed by Eggert Petersen and with the author as a member, has collected data since 1982 in connection with a project named *The Danes During the Crisis,* using surveys of a representative population of 2,000 above the age of fifteen. In 1988 (and in 1990) it became possible to include some questions on alcohol consumption in the survey. The fundamental analysis of the 1988-data is presented in the article. The article has been published in Hungarian in Additologia Hungaria, II, 2, 126-131, 1994.

3. **Social group patterns and alcohol consumption.** In this article, a continued analysis of the data from article two is carried out. A number of relevant cross-analyses are undertaken and the results considered in the perspective of what is called social consciousness in the article.

4. **Heavy consumption of alcohol and social groupings.** Again using data from the *Crisis project,* these are analysed from the perspective of heavy consumption. The aim of the article is to give a picture of the distribution of heavy consumers across the social groupings of society. The two articles, 3 and 4, are compiled into one in a Danish version which will be published in an anthology of *Crisis-project* research, expected summer 1994.

5. **Alcohol and work**. On account of a growing interest in alcohol and work it was decided to use data from the Consumer Consciousness-survey and undertake a first analysis of the relations. The results (from the *Danish* version) have been used by the labour market organizations and others in debates on alcohol policy in the workplace.

6. **Reasons for drinking/not drinking alcohol**. Besides the consumption questions the 1988-survey of the *Crisis Project* also had a couple of questions on reasons to drink/not to drink alcohol. These questions were presented in the survey as open questions, asking the respondent to name three reasons for each of the questions asked. The article originally was written as a background paper for a work-group at the *Nordic Alcohol Researcher Conference* in Iceland, 1990. In a *Danish* (slightly different) version, the article was published in *Skrifter fra Canfau*, 1 (2), 1992, and in Hungarian in Additologia Hungaria, II, 1, 7-14, 1994.

7. **Alcohol, low price, availability - increased consumption**. In discussing the analysis of the data from the *Consumer Consciousness*-survey it became evident that there was a possibility of examining aspects of the problem of border-trade. The article represents the result of an analysis of the relationship between price, availability and consumption with the division of the survey data into relevant regional categories. The article was published in Danish in *Nordisk Alkohol Tidskrift*, *1* (2), 1991 and in Hungarian in *Additologia Hungaria*, I, *2*, 106-110, 1993.

8. **Therapist consciousness**. One activity in the *Consumer Consciousness*-project was discussing the of development of the consciousness-concept. As a result of this, two ideas arose. One is documented in the analysis of a treatment/prevention system mentioned above (p. 2). The other was tried out in a student-research project under the supervision of the author. The result was a thesis (speciale) which was classified as confidential. On the basis of the data, an article was written by the supervisor and one of the students. Using the frame of understanding of the project it analyses the therapists and other groups in alcohol treatment/prevention work. On the initiative of researchers at Eötvös Lorand University, Budapest, the article was translated into *Hungarian*.

9. **Alcohol in society. The case of Denmark**. This final article overlaps other presentations in the volume to some extent, i.e. article 1, 2, 3, and 6. But the overlapping text has been partly rewritten and placed in a specific framework, which extends the previous presentations. The article is the result of a task

undertaken for the Amsterdam Group and was published in "Alcohol beverages and European Society, Annex 1." Its aims are to illustrate a beer-dominated drinking culture through consumption patterns, attitudes, traditions/rituals, and alcohol policy/prevention. The article offers a frame of understanding and suggests models and topics for research and prevention.

The *linking* factor of the eight articles is that they were all produced in relation to the project *The Danes' Alcohol Consumer Consciousness* even that articles 2, 3, 4, and 6 draw on data from the *Crisis project.* They were not written in succession or from a fixed point of departure, but the articles 2 to 7 and 9 represent different analyses of data from two major surveys which display a very coherent picture, a picture important when dealing with a perspective which has always been predominant in the project: Rational prevention thinking. It has been argued with persistence that no rational prevention - as opposed to a moral-oriented prevention - can be established without knowledge of the role alcohol plays in the daily life of a population and knowledge of the function that alcohol fulfils in a cultural perspective. The aim of the project was to provide such knowledge.

As a final introductory remark it should be mentioned that the articles have been altered or supplemented in relation to the presentation in this volume compared to previous presentations in different connections.

References

Elmeland, Karen, Nygaard, P. & Sabroe, K.-E. (1990). Storbrugere. 12 fortællinger om alkohol. *Psykologisk Skriftserie Aarhus*, 15, *1.*

Petersen, E, Andersen, J.G., Larsen, J.D., Sabroe, K.-E. & Sommerlund, B. (1989). *De krisebevidste og offervillige danskere.* Aarhus: Institute of Psychology. ('The crisis-conscious and self-sacrificing Danes')

Sabroe, K.-E. (1989). Alcohol Consumer Consciousness. A social psychological perspective on alcohol. Oslo: National Directorate for the Prevention of Alcohol and Drug Problems. *Proceedings 35th ICCA*, vol IV, 1-21.

Sabroe, K.-E. (1991). Alkohol, lav pris, tilgængelighed - øget forbrug? *Nordisk Alkohol Tidsskrift, 1, no. 2.* 73-80 ('Alcohol, low price, easy availability - increased consumption?')

Sabroe, K.-E. (1992) Grunde til at drikke/ikke at drikke alkohol. *Skrifter fra CANFAU*, 1, 2, 37-61. ('Reasons to drink/not to drink alcohol')

Sabroe, K.-E. (1993). Alkohol. Alacsony ár, hossá/erhetöseq - magasabb fogyaszatás. *Additologia Hungaria*, I, 2, 106-110.

Sabroe, K.-E. (1993). Alcohol in society. In *Alcohol beverages and European society*. Annex 1, section IV, 1-48.

Sabroe, K.-E. (1993). *Rusmiddelindsats på regionalt niveau*. Vejle: Vejle Amtskommune.

Sabroe, K.-E. (1994). A dánok alkoholfogyasztói tudatossága. *Additologia Hungaria*, II, 1, 7-14.

Sabroe, K.-E. (1994). Az alkoholfogyasztás es a tarsadalmi czoportok. *Additologia Hungaria*, II, 2, 126-131.

1.

ALCOHOL CONSUMER CONSCIOUSNESS

A social psychological perspective on alcohol

ALCOHOL CONSUMER CONSCIOUSNESS.
A social psychological perspective on alcohol

I Concepts and Frame of References

I.1 Introduction

The object of this paper is to argue for a social psychological frame of reference in the task of comprehending the relationship between man in his daily life and alcohol.

Emphasizing the psychology part of social psychology brings the individual into focus, and a major part of this paper will deal with consciousness as an individual phenomenon. But although the individual is in focus, a major concern for a social psychologist will also be the question of which social institutions within society are the important bearers of the alcohol culture, is it the family, peer-groups, work groups, larger (political/religious) groupings? Which social mechanisms sustain the alcohol culture, are they norms, rules, values, formal laws? And why and how does the specific alcohol culture change?

Although the bio-medical research and epidemological research account for most alcohol research, important research in the tradition of sociology-ethnography-social antrophology, the attempts to establish the relationship between culture and drinking behaviour has developed during the last three decades (Pittman & Snyder, 1962; Everett, Wadell & Heath, 1976; Marshall, 1979; Room, 1979; Paakkanen & Sulkunen, 1987). A major point of view in this tradition is the assumed existence of various nation - stereotypes, among which are national traditions of drinking alcohol and national ways of regarding the effects of alcohol consumption. It is so obvious a fact, that even the layman would be able to provide evidence of this assumption from his experience as a tourist. That such differences have a long history is argued by Segal (1986) in his discussion of Soviet and American culture. An early Danish source is provided by professor in medicine Ole Worm (1652) who in his 'Controversium Medicarum Excercitatio XVIII' states that "... *beer* for the Nordic people is a common and healthy drink, and owing to the beer our countrymen are healthier, stronger and more beautiful than those who through continuos *wine*-drinking dry out the intestines, shrivel the blood-mass and makes the constitution of the body more spare and weak" (cit. Hovesen, 1987). If we weight historical evidence, this seems to modify the Mäkelä (1986) statement that alcohol in Scandinavia is not part of the daily meal, not part of daily social life, but is isolated to specific situations with intoxication as the dominant function. But this has not always been the case, and my postulate is that this description of the Scandinavians must at least exclude the Danes, which in the common use of beer are in line with their historic origins, in accordance with Worm's statement.

Cultural traditions also embrace preferred type of alcohol, consumption patterns, drinking places and companions. National characteristics are, however, not an indication of a consensus in behaviour, attitude etc. Various 'aspects of culture' and their manifestations may well represent the same underlying culture. Within nations there may be differences between subgroups that are more marked than those between equal social strata in two different nations, and this applies not only to multi-ethnic societies such as the USA and the USSR. In spite of these subgroup differences the nation-characteristic is identifiable, and we would say as a *'national alcohol consumption consciousness'*, others may think of it in terms of *'conscience collectives'* in the tradition of Durkheim (Sabroe, 1984). In geographical-economic research the concept of *regional consciousness* sometimes is applied and used in a way similar to that just expressed (Rejkiel, 1985).

But again contrary to these differences between nations there are developmental patterns across nations which are homogenous over periods of time. For western/industrialized societies parallel developments for instance have occurred with regard to an increase in consumption, decline of age for start, extension of the area of use in daily life (societal and with regard to place) and new patterns of preferred type of alcohol, equalization of sexual differences, patterns which either change or become incremental to old patterns.

1.2 Research and Prevention

In previous research alcohol to a great extent has been treated in connection with the development towards or treatment of alcoholism, or in connection with abuse, addiction and the extreme situation known as intoxication. The end *product* of an inappropriate relationship man-alcohol-society thus seems more predominant than the rational *process* in which man unproblematically relates to alcohol/society. In the 'Great Danish Dictionary' the word *intoxication* is clearly defined as referring to a situation, in which behaviour is inappropriate and is result of a 'distorted' consciousness. In contrast to the bulk of treatment, addiction, alcoholism research there is far less research regarding the alcohol-induced condition called *ecstasy* or (*joyful*) *drunkeness*. This condition is characterized as a situation in which the individual's customary relations with his/her surroundings are affected, but without necessarily leading to inappropriate behaviour. Nor is there much research regarding the impact of alcohol in daily life, of alcohol relishing behaviour, which precedes the ecstasy, and which is the behaviour characteristic of the great majority of alcohol consumption in Danish society at least.

Can we adequately explain the progress up to the ecstasy situation, and can we learn to use signals which maintain the ecstasy and prevent the inappropriateness of intoxication? In connection with prevention, such knowledge would of course be of the utmost importance. But broadly speaking the ultimate goal must be to bring about a development towards a situation in which alcohol in society and in daily life of the individual *does not* appear as a segregated subject with a problematic character, *but* is experienced as a subject among others, i.e. harmoniously integrated in culture/way of life.

This - as stated - is evidently the case for the majority of the Danish population. But the grey area starting at the high consumer end of the majority of 'normal' drinkers and extending into the small minority group of abusive drinkers is of a sufficient size to consider a broadly aimed but rational prevention. The precondition for this is a thorough knowledge of how alcohol is represented in the minds of men in the specific society.

It was previously stated that a preoccupation with alcohol as '*an evil*' has dominated research especially within the bio-medical tradition, but also the sociological-anthropological research to some extent. But that alcohol can do harm, that biological and physiological damage occur when abuse is present, that societal and social psychological consequences can be the result of excessive consumption and that individual psychological problems accompany over-indulgence in alcohol, are historically and scientifically documented.

As has been pointed out by many national and international agencies - first and foremost the WHO - there is a trend in these cross-national developments, which does a preventive effort indispensable. But support for prevention and similar actions has often taken form of a moralistic crusade, in which 'the evil' (alcohol) is the target and where considerations regarding the circumstances, which make the substance 'an evil' have also followed moralistic-political lines.

From a psychological point of view such types of prevention will seldom be considered appropriate. One reason for this is that moralistic approaches towards human behaviour often - though of course not always - carry with them a depreciation of the given behaviour, and stigma is an obvious possibility. The main target of a moralistic approach is the emotions and mostly exclude the human intellect, disregard the cognitive potential of being able to act on the basis of reflected knowledge.

The alternative, accomplishing rational/humanistic prevention, is not easily achieved. You do not have the ready answers of the moralist and the simple models of man and society, and if you want to involve the capacities of human mind you must have knowledge of it not only at a general level, but also of the actual historic consciousness, its structure and content. From our existing knowledge it is apparent that subjects such as availability, control, attitude to alcohol consumption and to alcohol related problems are important. Data regarding these areas can be derived from official data, laws, police regulations, public orders etc. These make up a highly complex picture as illustrated below (fig. 1):

Fig. 1: Alcohol in society

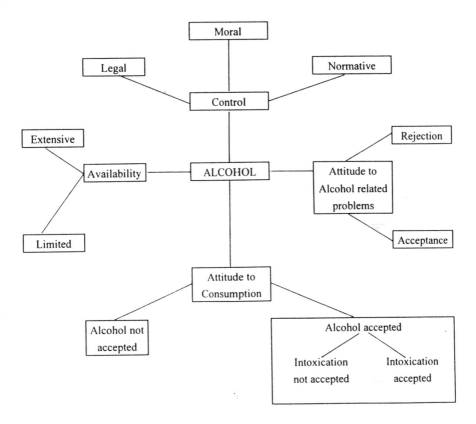

The four areas are of course not a complete description of the way a society relates to the subject of alcohol and the diagram does not bring out the interrelationship between the areas, but they are significant factors, and can be regarded as core elements in what could be termed the 'national alcohol consumption consciousness'.

An attempt to describe the relationship between two of the areas in a matrix using quantity as a measure could have the form of figure 2:

Figure 2: Alcohol Availability/Control Matrix

	Alcohol Availability	
	limited	extensive
minimum	Countries with 'no' alcohol tradition	Countries with liberal attitudes
Alcohol Control		
maximum	Countries with severe restrictions or prohibition	Countries with strict normative systems

In any attempt to create preventive actions, knowledge of the areas in fig. 1 is inevitable, but to reiterate, no thorough understanding is possible without taking the *individual* alcohol comsumption consciousness into consideration.

I.3 Alcohol in Society

Alcohol is a product of society, a product which consumated affects the CNS, and thus affects the individual's perception of his/her surroundings and of him/herself. The basis for the individual's behaviour is thus changed, but there is no one-way relationship between the influence on the CNS and the resulting behaviour. Different psychic 'mechanisms' - conditioned by the impact of culture in its broadest sense and of specific learning - are 'regulating' the concrete behaviour. In a historic perspective alcohol has displayed an incessant existence, and it has a relatively pronounced placing with regard to dissemination and extent in many societies. Against this background drinking alcohol has - by cultural tradition - been a ready-action possibility in coping with life-situations. And this readiness will be transformed into use by the socially underpriviledged or those who are stressed because of heavy responsibilities, when you are emotionally down or in states of excitement or other extremes. But in many societies it is also a common subject in 'daily life' or for conviviality, and for the vast majority of the members of society, a *'cultural immunity'* (Schiøler, 1987) ensures that a cultural rationality is characteristic of the man-alcohol relationship.

Alcohol drinking as a subject is surrounded by a great number of myths and rituals, and various attitudes and values are attached to drinking. Myths and rituals are most often independent of the individual, but attitudes and values are personal prerequisites with which the individual enters the drinking situation. As shown in figure 3, these prerequisites, together with the conception 'the situation after the situation' are central in the understanding of the individual's behaviour. Figure 3 is an attempt to outline what could be called 'situation-oriented alcohol consumer consciousness'. What I named personal requisites amount to more than, but also include, the individual's (general) alcohol consumer consciousness. In stressing the drinking situation perspective I have found it appropriate to emphasize the importance of the two factors 'previous experiences' and 'the nearest future' as determinative on the individual's side. But one cannot arrive at an understanding of drinking behaviour solely from the individual. Alcohol consumption is a behaviour with which the individual relates to society, therefore 'alcohol as subject in society' and 'experienced actual life situation' are important framefactors. And it is very important to remember that all alcohol understanding must set out from 'alcohol as subject in society'. It cannot stand alone though, because the way in which alcohol presents itself as a subject is dependent on the processing, the individual members of society undertake, and the general and specific characteristics of this processing.

Figure 3: Situation oriented alcohol consumer consciousness

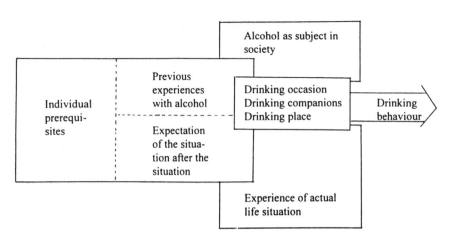

In accentuating the situation perspective importance is attached to what is in focus for the individual and this means that the concept of awareness becomes essential. But it is important not to confuse though the two concepts consciousness and awareness (cf. section I.5).

In figure 1 and the text above the concept, *Alcohol Consumer Consciousness* has been introduced. In the next section, the concept of consciousness is elaborated a little further.

I.4 The Concept of Consciousness

A major wish in the development of psychology has always been to find the primary concept which can explain comprehensively and indisputably the *relationship* between the individual and his/her surroundings. One such concept has been attitude and motive, need, drive, trait have been others. Consciousness is not a competitor to these concepts, but the accentuation of the consciousness perspective attempts to call attention to the wholeness of the human mind and of the continuity and coherence, which are characteristic of the lives of individuals and to the life in human institutions, first and foremost the family and other primary groups. Consciousness is experienced by the individual as a *wholeness* which unites the multitude of cognitions, emotions and perceptions of the outer world. Consciousness is an ongoing and ever-changing human activeness. Through the active perception of his/her surroundings the individual acquires material which is the foundation of his/her behaviour. The understanding of and the wish to be able to *predict* this behaviour has always been predominant, all the way back to the period in human evolution in which the human mind becomes a conscious mind, that is when man realizes that there is an *objective* world independent of the subject, when the mind becomes *intentional/purpose* oriented and when the mind acquires the capability to *reflect* on itself. With the concept of consciousness - understood as the individual's acquisition of reality - we have taken a starting point in the uniquely human in a twofold sense. Partly, it is consciousness which differentiates us from animals, and it is partly the consciousness in its particular form that differentiates human individuals from each other.

Consciousness can thus - from an individual psychological perspective - be defined as the state of mind in which the individual relates *cognitively* and *emotionally* to him- or herself and to his or her social and physical environment. Consciousness in this sense signifies a uniqueness, maybe *the uniqueness* of mental life. Consciousness is a phenomenon which it is impossible to break down into other components or define by anything else. Nor is consciousness something which emerges out of nothing. It is the totality of 'experiences' that are acquired in the process of man's relating to his surroundings, it is a relationship between an individual and objects in its widest sense (i.e. material and immaterial objects including him- or herself). It is important to understand consciousness as a *relationship* to the environment, which we come to know about through the (conscious) experiences, which we share with other human beings. Consciousness is a necessary functional aspect of our dialectic relationship with the environment, necessary for the individual to sustain life.

As a characteristic of human life consciousness, as defined, can on the one hand refer to the specific capability of the human being to experience the stream of life consciously, the precondition for his activeness (in German equal to Bewusstsein). On the other hand it is also used to characterize the peculiar way in which the individual relates to his stream of life, to signify the individual, subjective quality of the activeness or modes of action (in German equal to Bewusstheit).

These two modes of consciousness never fall into well-defined classes, but are rather positions in a passive-active dimension (Hilgard, 1980). One important subject in studying these modes will therefore be *attention,* which in this connection can be regarded as an aspect of 'controlling' consciousness. Consciousness is a foundation of the individual's relationship to reality, and these relationships have the character of (*life-*)*activeness*, which is necessary for the individual's life-maintenance.

It is therefore the active mode with which we are mostly concerned as it is characteristic of the way in which the individual articulates his/her life. As human beings we are always acting. Human consciousness is thus part of the individuals' experience, as his/her personal way of being-in-the world. Moncrieff (1978) states that consciousness is

> *"...a matrix of human wonder and all that such wonder can lead us to discover. It is our openness to whatever can be relevant to us and our sense of that relevance achieved" (p.359).*

Consciousness is a constituent in the creation of meaning. Moncrieff (ibid) says that phenomenologists refer to this by saying that consciousness is *intentional.* By stating that consciousness is a constituent in the creation of meaning, we have taken a decisive step towards the use of consciousness as a characteristic of the individual's articulation of his/her life activity.

Consciousness, conceived as the individuals' intentional dealing with the stream of life (making meaning of life), is related to the concept of attitude. And both of these concepts are used in psychological theory as characterizing the basis for taking a position towards life events.

An investigation of consciousness must necessarily reflect *the intentionality* which is a predominant feature of it, indicating that it is an active processing of something in the surroundings or of itself, as we shall see later.

Another aspect of consciousness is that when we express ourselves or react in life situations there is a certain *consistency*, a rationally accentuated coherence, and within certain limits it is possible to predict an individual's behaviour. Our consciousness has - generally considered - a certain *rationality*, which is expressed in the acts we implement in our interaction with our surroundings in order to obtain control over our conditions of life. But exactly because we are human beings, the wording 'a certain rationality' is important, because seen in spe cific connections the individual's behaviour could be seen as apparently irrational with regard to 'set' goals.

A third condition is that our consciousness is *reflexive*, we have a self-consciousness. It has already been hinted above that we react to ourselves as we react with regard to conditions in our surroundings. When we look at our behaviour, the reaction in relation to ourselves is always retrospective, even though the self-consciousness as 'stored information' can be a link in an antecedent regulation of this behaviour.

Consciousness is thus given 'eo ipso', what it is consciousness of, it is intentional and not mechanically determined. But as also indicated consciousness is not anything in its own right either, it is the result of man's societal being. Society is the foundation from which the human mind has its content, and are essentially the symbol systems which offer a structuring of human thinking and interhuman relationships. Through these symbol systems the *meaning-bearing* perceptions which are the basis of human behaviour are established. Consciousness and behaviour are thus of a piece in the sense that meaning-bearing perceptions 'motivate' the individual's acting. Research in the concept of meaning therefore becomes important because it is the basis of human action and interrelations.

Consciousness is always being conscious of something, and this something has a common content in the individual culture/society, but also to a great extent across cultures, and it applies to both material and immaterial subjects. Material subjects have an existence in their own right, but one can talk about an existence in their own right for many immaterial subjects (with relation to the individual). But as subjects they are incorporated and processed by the individual into a personal functional base. Within a given culture the general - in relationship to these subjects - sets the framework, but within this, shades and differences of meaning are established by the individual.

This is reflected in the existence of attitudes, meanings, emotions and inclinations to act, in relation to the fact that alcohol exists in a given society. For instance important areas of research will be: Why have the prevailing attitudes and inclinations of acting with regard to alcohol developed? Why (when and how) is alcohol selected 'to cope with' the situations of life? How are the attitudes/ways of acting maintained, how is change brought about? It is important in this connection to remember that attitudes are not motivating, but are considered as a hypothetic intervening variable governing the relationship between the individual and his surroundings. Attitudes are a construct which answer the question of 'what' (content) of this relation. Attitudes cannot be seen as the cause of the individual's alcohol behaviour for example, attitudes are to a great extent the individual's choice of 'explanation' of such thing as the concrete alcohol behaviour, and attitudes are above all based on experience (Sabroe, 1984).

I.5 Consciousness and Awareness

The introduction of Alcohol Consumer Consciousness can be seen as an attempt to overcome some of the confusion regarding the existing concepts in the field of alcohol research within the tradition of social psychology, sociology and anthropology. Related and often synonymously used concepts would be values, ideology, attitudes, beliefs, opinions, frames of reference and so on. Attitudes, beliefs and opinions have often been used in research projects with a social or psychological perspective, and a common result has been, that there seems to be a correspondance between the attitudes expressed about drinking behaviour and the individual's specific drinking behaviour, but rather weaker relationships between attitudes towards broader alcohol related subjects such as alcoholism and abstinence and the specific behaviour (McCarthy et al., 1983). This is a subject which has been taken up in the everlasting discussion on the connection between expressed attitudes and behaviour towards the subject in question. Recent research has drawn attention to the fact that the lack of accordance often found in research including general or broad subjects to a great extent disappears when attitudes and behaviour towards more specific subjects are compared, indicating that the discrepancy seems more to be a methodological problem than an expression of a real inconsistency between attitude and behaviour (Sabroe, 1984, ch. 4).

Within the concept of Alcohol Consumer Consciousness we are trying to see attitudes and behaviour as integrated features of man's relationship to alcohol. Instead of trying to establish a relationship between the respondent's experienced behaviour and some measure of attitude towards alcohol, which is a product of the mind of the research team, we are trying to *find out* how - giving an open opportunity - the individual will express him-/herself concerning this behaviour. This is a very crucial point in our theoretical and methodological approach to the field of alcohol research. We will attempt to place greater emphasis on finding out what people think about their drinking than to test our own way of thinking regarding drinkers. This point of view follows from Alfred Schutz's distinction between 'common-sense knowledge' and 'scientific knowledge'. According to

Schutz (1974) the social world has a specific meaning and relevance for the people who live in it. They navigate through their daily life with the help of common-sense constructions. And they make their decisions and form their behaviour upon these common-sense constructions.

Parallel to ordinary people making common-sense-constructions, we have the scientists (according to Schutz) who try to figure out or make scientific constructions of the social world. We do not of course consider the scientific construction attitude towards social phenomena as futile and we believe that applying the Alcohol Consumer Consciousness, as our concept of 'what is in the mind of people' and using the mentioned strategy of collecting and analyzing data will give a better knowledge of man and alcohol and thereby a more adequate basis for future work along the line of rational prevention.

Consciousness meaning: The specific way the individual relates to his stream of life can be said to be a phenomenon, which he utilizes to a greater or lesser degree. A systematization along these lines would be:

As we see it one could relate to life in a way where things are simply passing by. One does not make up one's mind about one's acts and more or less reflexively relate to one's own demands or those of one's surroundings; we could call it a state of *passive consciousness* (or low degree of consciousness). Even when brought to the attention it is difficult specifically to identify the intention or meaning of any given act, or to give signifying characteristics.

In other situations one could be described as being in a state of *adaptive consciousness*. It is a situation in which decisions have been involved in the life acts, but these decisions are more or less automatic reactions adjusted to the challenges one meets in the specific situation. Brought to attention, the challenge and reaction can be combined and even after-rationalized.

Another mode is an *active consciousness* (or high degree of consciouss) which is characterized by reflected actions in the situation and with antecedent processing of future situations, using knowledge and previous experiences. There is an extreme awareness of the here and now but always as a reflected moment in the individual's continuous constructive effort to control the life situations, in the individual's development as a human being*.

---

* I am indebted for this division of the concept is in debt to the crisis research carried out at the Institute of Psychology (Petersen, E., Sabroe, K.-E., Kristensen, O.S., Sommerlund, B. (1987).

The use of the concept of consciousness may, however, create a problem for us. The choice of the concept was based on my native language, Danish, and on the Danish psychological tradition. But as we know there are slight differences between languages in the denotations and often greater differences in the connotations of a given word which broadly speaking relates to the same phenomenon, and this is the case both in everyday language and when these words are transferred into scientific concepts. In discussions with colleagues from especially English-speaking countries it has come to my attention that the clearly positive value placed in the Danish 'at være bevidst om...' is not necessarily as prevalent in the English 'to be conscious of ...'. In Danish 'being conscious' definitely means more than being aware, and is regarded as an active mode based on reflection (on cognitions and emotions). Another problem exists with regard to translations from languages of Latin origin into Anglo/German/Nordic languages. In French 'la conscience' means both *consciousness* and *conscience*. This may, of course, create problems in applying the term, although my opinion is that the positive connotations mentioned above can be readily accepted, when pointed out. So I have no hesitation continuing to argue for its use.

Consciousness is a unique phenomenon. In discussions in international seminars the question has sometimes been asked if awareness would not be a better term than consciousness. And in fact one finds the concepts of consciousness and awareness used synonymously. This is not appropriate, not only in a scientific sense, but also according to Webster's Oxford dictionary of the English language for example, in which the two words clearly differ in their denotations. Awareness is a more restricted concept than consciousness and is related to consciousness as focus is to perspective. I shall not pursue the language differences or the confusion between the daily use and the scientific use, which I think has been the main reason behind the problem regarding awareness and consciousness. In short, I will describe the way *we* see the two concepts:

Consciousness is a concept relating to totality. It is the continuous readiness, it is what is *potentially* available to us, as our conscious activeness.

Awareness is the actual field of attention, it is a restricted field, the specific subject among the conceivable, which *for the moment* occupies the major activity of the mind.

Danskernes tilværelse under krisen I-II. Aarhus: Aarhus Universitetsforlag. ('Danes during the Crisis'). There is also a certain relationship to Hilgard's presentation (Hilgard, E. (1980) Consciousness. *Annual Review Psychology*, vol. *31*, 1-13.

II   A Research Project

II.1 Introduction

In this second part of the paper I shall deal with a concrete research project established at the Institute of Psychology, University of Aarhus, Denmark.

The *Alcohol Research Group* project at the Institute of Psychology, University of Aarhus, concerning the concept *'Alcohol Consumer Consciousness'* (ACC) had, so to speak, a headlong start. The fact is that up to 1987 there was no alcohol oriented research at the Institute, though in the early seventies there was a certain interest for research on narcotics behaviour (Katzenelson, 1973; 1974a&b). But through an extensive research on reaction to crises and on attitudes (Petersen et al., 1987; 1989) a foundation ready when the opportunity to apply general psychological theory to the area of alcohol research came along. This readiness supplemented with ideas (Schiøler, 1987) from the chief consultant on alcohol and drugs to the Ministry of Research and Education, also became an important factor when the first outline of the project was established. It very rapidly became evident that the frame of understanding which ought to be applied was that of the psychology of normal behaviour.

This decision was reached with the help of three sets of information. *First,* a fast review of titles in the research area proved that the majority of research was biomedically oriented, and concerned mainly with the *'victim'* of alcohol. *Second* it appeared that the research within the areas of clinical psychology and sociology/anthropology which - especially regarding the latter - dealt with patterns and customs of drinking behaviour, was also more interested in 'unusual' behaviour than in 'normal' behaviour. *Third* the application of the intended research as a means of a better understanding of what to do in (a rational) prevention of an individually and socially damaging consumption of alcohol pointed, at 'normal' behaviour as the target of investigation.

Taking worry as the point of departure seems to have been common to much research and research on 'normal' consumption of alcohol was lacking. If we ignore the data obtained from research concerned with amounts consumed and consumption patterns. A psychologist, and especially a social psychologist, must always ask the question *why?*, when presented with such data, especially when he/she goes beyond the actual figures and looks at the changes over time. Such changes are connected with broader societal alterations, manifesting themselves in altered general values and norms and describable through these, but it must be evident that no thorough knowledge can be obtained unless one understands the structure and content of what we have called the individual's 'Alcohol Consumer Consciousness'. No simple linear model can be assumed however, the individual and society are in a dialectic relationship, each determining the other.

On the basis of the reasoning above we thus arrived at a four point conclusion, namely:

1. That research into alcohol related problems ought to be as broad as possible, interdisciplinary and cross-cultural.

2. That it is important for the research to take the perspective of the individual.

3. That the goal of the research should be to establish a foundation for promoting conscious behaviour towards alcohol, and

4. That the task of establishing the individual's experiences with and how he/she relates to alcohol should be based on a phenomenological method.

The study of the consciously acting individual cannot be undertaken with a simple frame of understanding (f.ex. a S-R model). Meaningful perceptions and intentional actions must be included in the understanding. The point of departure must be the individual and his/her experiences of his/her surroundings. When the individual has experiences with alcohol, alcohol is not experienced in a 'pure sense', but is interpreted and are having social meaning. Alcohol becomes part of the definition of the social situation.

Both in the industrialized and developing countries the experience of the environment is characterized by a continuous progression. But a major problem is that our chance of predicting the next position on the curve of progression is poor. Yet the experience embodied in the world picture, or more specifically in the alcohol consumer consciousness, is important to us, because it serves important functions, as well as being the model we have of the reality: Alcohol in society. It provides a frame of understanding for the essential conditions of man's relationship to alcohol and it becomes the 'legitimate' foundation for our acting with alcohol in social life. And thereby also the foundation for surviving life crises in which alcohol starts becoming important. Again, this stresses the importance of an active consciousness as defined above and the only way to achieve that with regard to alcohol seems to be rational prevention, indicating that an open-minded and unprejudiced education is imperative. It is our firm belief that people in a normal state of mind do not consciously destroy themselves, and consequently that enhanced consciousness leads to mental and physical health.

A couple of times - also in the last paragraph - the concept rational prevention has been used. When prevention is used with the adjective rational, it should be understood in a broader sense than in its traditionel use within medicine, where it is narrowly related to illness. Prevention in this connection is understood as a wide area of thinking and acting towards a life totality. It is obvious that if we take prevention in its narrow meaning, we could ask if the effort inherent in the project is necessary, when at the most ten per cent of the population is in a situation in which the consumption of alcohol is a health risk. But *when* we, with the concept of prevention, aim not only at the marginal ten per cent but also wish to include the dark grey area in which alcohol consumption is not an immediate personal or social life risk, but is a potential danger which may drastically impair or destroy the person's own or his relations' life quality, or include the lighter grey area where the consumption of alcohol has become a 'not-conscious' activity with consequences for relationships to family, work or other areas, *then* a thorough knowledge is necessary, and the effort to obtain population representative information is worthwhile and essential. If we are going to establish a (rational) prevention on the basis of the broader understanding of the concept prevention, we must necessarily have a thorough knowledge regarding the area towards which the prevention is directed. We cannot establish prevention on diffuse suppositions. We must have a specific foundation, first and foremost a knowledge of the Alcohol Consumer Consciousness.

II. 2 Social Relations from the Perspective of the Individual

Social psychology must always pay attention to the balancing act between psychological reductionism and sociological determinism. But as already hinted above, we seek to overcome this difficulty by concentrating on the relationship thus remaining aware of both the social aspect and the individual. Fundamental to the thinking of social psychology is that man is actively creating his environment as well as being affected by it. It is important always to remember, however, that the influence from society is conveyed through the human being. In this process the human being always appears with a set of prerequisites for dealing with the impact from society.

The concept of the individual's Alcohol Consumer Consciousness' (ACC) was first presented by Sabroe (1986). In ibid., the concept *preliminary* was defined as a hypothetical construction, an intervening variable which counts for the readiness on the individual's part for the interaction between the individual and society. It was further stated that the ACC was based on experience and that cognitive-, emotional- and action-oriented elements all played a major role. Structurally it was supposed that the actual experienced life situation, objective, stable cultural factors and experienced personal conditions were among the essential factors. Broadly speaking, the main core of Alcohol Consumer Consciousness refers to the way in which the individual relates (thinks, feels, acts) to the substance alcohol and to its use individually and in society.

In Sabroe & Rasmussen (1987, 1988) this argumentation was further developed. By establishing the project "Alcohol Consumer Consciousness" it became obvious to us, that we were "breaking new ground" and that previous knowledge was not readily available. We very soon became aware that with the idea of the ACC we had opened up a complex of problems that we could not hope fully to come to terms with within the scope and time available for the first part of the project. The frame of understanding which has governed our way of thinking and which is outlined in part one should thus be regarded as a working hypothesis rather than an established theoretical understanding.

The objective of the project is to obtain a thorough and psychologically relevant understanding of ACC. We wish to come to an understanding of the meaning of alcohol within the context of human existence. We want to know which conditions constitute the ACC. ACC cannot be apprehended in isolation. The achievement of obtaining an understanding of the meaning of alcohol for the individual is to get hold of a system of relationships or a pattern which is connected to other patterns in all parts of the culture of daily life. To understand ACC it is necessary to understand the way in which the individual comes to terms with work, family, leisure and the way these areas of life are embedded in society.

The conceptions of alcohol and alcohol consumption which prevail in a society are a societal product and are historically defined. The content is a function of the consciousness the individual carries of society and its development and of society's evaluation and preoccupation with the concept of alcohol. People's conceptions are a manifestation of the history of society. And the conceptions are societal phenomena, specific to the culture of the society.

In European countries alcohol and alcohol consumption differ in importance and have different values both in the societal and the scientific debate. Thus it must be important in an understanding of the ACC relevant to our historical period to accomplish cross cultural studies. This could be fruitful both with regard to theory/understanding and methodology/empirical evidence.

As already stated the underlying approach in the project is eclectic social psychological. Being social psychological means that it is the active human being as he/she exists in society, his/her relations and reactions to the social world which is the target of theorizing and empirical investigation. In Sabroe (1984) the social psychological point of view is defined as, from the standpoint of the individual, to try to come to an understanding of how and why he or she relates to society as a whole, to its institutions, organizations, groups and cultural products and to his/her fellow man in the way he/she does. Alcohol as a cultural product is a subject to relate to and is quite an important subject in our societies. It might even be called a dominant one; it is there with a consequence that forces one to make up one's mind about it.

Asplund (1987) argues that the elementary form of social behaviour is 'social responsitivity' and 'responsive sociality'. This understanding is also important from the social psychological point of view, introduced above. 'Social responsitivity' is fundamental. It cannot be reduced to anything else. And it is the foundation for the prerequisites previously mentioned. These ways of reacting towards a subject will moreover be determined by non-systematically overtaken traditions and systematically acquired knowledge.

The overall purpose of the present research project is to gain new knowledge of the common use of alcohol, of alcohol as a subject in the existence of the ordinary man's daily life, - in short to get knowledge about the ACC of 'the Dane'. But the applicational aspect of this knowledge is also important, and could preliminarily be stated as the goal of increased ACC. This is not just an understanding of the individual's own use of alcohol, the specific 'what', 'when', 'where', 'how' and 'why' of this use. It is also an acknowledgement of the existence of a common knowledge, an understanding of alcohol as a phenomenon of daily life, of the function of alcohol in human relations and of the particular position of alcohol in our own and other cultures. The ultimate understanding will also include the comprehension of the importance of the economic conditions, which are related to the production, distribution and taxation of alcohol.

II.3 Methodology

An important subject in all empirical science is the theory-methodology relationship and, in preparing the project, an existentialistic-phenomenological theoretical orientation has played a major part. And of course the research group are psychologists and first and foremost social psychologists. This means that in dealing with alcohol it is not the substance alcohol and its attributes which have our interest, but the relationship between the substance alcohol and the human beings. It is not alcohol in isolation but alcohol as it is experienced in relation to human life we find important. This also means that in taking the theory-method connection seriously, we have tried *not* to impose ourselves on the data field.

Our conclusion is that the individual acts in the world in accordance with his understanding of the world, i.e. the particular meaning the world has for him. Further we will conclude that we cannot know what alcohol and the use of alcohol means to a population until we have studied the whole subject of alcohol from the perspective of the individual. But as Schutz (1971) points out, this concept of different perspectives (the subjective perspective and the perspective of the observer) does not imply that we are unable to grasp the reality of the world, but it does mean that we grasp only certain aspects of reality according to our knowledge, our interests and our position regarding this reality. About the "scientific perspective", Schutz (1971) says that,

> *"...all scientific explanations of the social world can, and for certain purposes must, refer to the subjective meaning of the actions of human beings from which social reality originates."(p.62)*

The vast majority of studies in the field of alcohol, that we have knowledge of, have been concerned, not with the perspective of the individual, but with the perspective of the observer (the scientist) studying behaviour and habits. We will not discard the observer's perspective, but the main task will be to describe and analyze the aspects of alcohol use from the perspective of the individual user.

The daily life of man, Schutz says, proceeds in a social, intersubjective world which is taken for granted. Apparently Schutz has in mind a picture of an individual who is able to drop into the state that Schutz calls the "epoché of the natural attitude" where reality is not questioned:

> *"this world existed before our birth, experienced and interpreted by others, our predecessors, as an organized world. Now it is given to our experience and interpretation. All interpretation of this world is based on a stock of previous experiences of it, our own or those handed down to us by parents or teachers; these experiences in the form of "knowledge at hand" function as a scheme of reference." (p.7)*

Schutz introduces the concept of "knowledge at hand" or "stock of knowledge" which consists of typifications of the common-sense world. Hereby Schutz actually restricts the knowledge of the individual to generalized or "semantic knowledge" (Tulving 1983) whereas the kind of knowledge that Tulving calls "episodic knowledge" and "procedural knowledge" does not seem to be included:

> *"The unquestioned pre-experiences are ... also from the outset, at hand as typical, that is, as carrying open horizons of anticipated similar experiences. For example, the outer world is not experienced as an arrangement of individual unique objects, dispersed in space and time, but as "mountains", "trees", "animals", "fellow-men"." (Schutz 1971 pp. 7,8)*

The Alcohol Consumption Consciousness of the individual can be conceptualized partly within Schutz' "stock of knowledge". We will not reduce this knowledge to generalized or semantic knowledge, however, but include all of the individual's knowledge and prerequisites for acting within the "world of alcohol". This would include skills, feelings, expectations, factual knowledge, conscious thoughts etc., as well as mind processes which the individual is not necessarily consciously aware of.

Our aim at doing is to attempt to get hold of the common-sense-constructions which are related to the use of alcohol and to let these findings substitute 'ad hoc' scientific constructions of beliefs and attitudes. This requires that the data collecting instruments must be adapted to absorb more 'qualitative' kinds of responses. The overall design of the data collecting instruments must be changed from the traditional quantitative and precoded design to a more qualitative design with room for answers which are not prestructured. Preliminary tests of qualitative designs have showed rather promising results, using telephones for the interview and computer technology for instant recording of data and statements. We have of course selected the topics that we want to investigate and which we find relevant to cover the alcohol consumption consciousness. But we have not used the scientific perspective and defined the frame within which the subjects are to give their answers. We have chosen to let the subject, on the stimuli, define their own frame of reference and openly from his understanding of the world express the reactions, which the stimuli provoke. It seems that people are quite ready to react to the open ended question, and the acquired data have already given us information that we could not have hoped to obtain if we had established our scientists preview as the frame of reference, within which the subjects could react.

REFERENCES

Ajzen, I. & Fishbein, M. (1977) Attitude - behavior relations. *Psychological Bulletin, 84*, 888-918.

Asplund, J. (1987) *Det sociala livets elementära former.* Göteborg: Korpen.

Everett, C.; Wadell, B. & Heath, D.B. (Eds.) (1976) *Cross cultural approaches to the study of alcohol*, New York: Morton Publishers.

Hilgard, E. (1980). Consciousness. *Annual Review Psychology, 31*, 1-13.

Hovesen, E. (1987) *Lægen Ole Worm.* Århus: Aarhus Universitetsforlag.

Katzenelson, B. (1973). *Forklaringsforsøg I.* København: Munksgaard.

Katzenelson, B. (1974a). *Forklaringsforsøg II.* København: Munksgaard.

Katzenelson, B. (1974b). *Stofproblemer.* København: Munksgaard.

Marshall, M. (Ed.) (1979) *Beliefs, behavior and alcohol beverages.* Ann Arbor: Michigan Univ. Press.

Mäkelä, K. (1986) Attitudes towards drinking and drunkenness in four Scandinavian countries. In Babor, T. (Ed.) *Alcohol and Culture.* New York: Annuals of the N.Y. Academy of Sciences, vol. 472.

McCarthy, D., Morrison, S. & Mills. K.C. (1983) Attitudes, Beliefs and Alcohol Use. *Journals of Studies on Alcohol, 44*, No. 2, 328-341.

Moncrieff, D.W. 1978. Aesthetic Consciousness. In: Valle R.S. and King M. (Eds.): *Existential-Phenomenological Alternatives for Psychology.* New York: Oxford Univ. Press.

Paakkanen, P. & Sulkunen, P. (1987). *Cultural studies on drinking and drinking problems.* Helsinki: Social Research Institute of Alcohol Studies.

Petersen, E., Sabroe, K.-E., Kristensen, O.S.. & Sommerlund, B. (1987). *Danskernes tilværelse under krisen. I-II.* Aarhus: Aarhus Universitetsforlag.

Pittman, D. J. & Snyder, C.R. (Eds.) (1962) *Society, Culture and Drinking Patterns*, New York: Wiley.

Regan, D.T. & Fazio, R.H. (1977) On the consistency between attitude and behavior. *Journ. Exp. Soc. Psych., 13*, 28-45.

Rejkiel, Z. (1985) Regional consciousness in the Katowice Region, Poland. *Area*, 17.4, 285-93.

Room, R. (1979) Priorities in Social Science Research on Alcohol. *Journal of Studies of Alcohol*, suppl. 8, 248-265.

Sabroe, K.-E. (1983) *Forelæsninger i socialpsykologi*. Aarhus: Psykologisk Institut, mimeo, 316 p. ('Lectures on social psychology')

Sabroe, K.E. (1984) *Socialpsykologi*, København: Akademisk Forlag.

Sabroe, K.-E. (1986) *The user consciousness of alcohol among the Danish population*. Århus: Institute of Psychology, mimeo, 21 p.

Sabroe, K.-E., Rasmussen, O. (1987) *Progress Report II*, Århus: Alcohol Research Group, mimeo, 17 p.

Sabroe, K.-E. & Rasmussen, O. (1988) *Progress Report III*. Aarhus: Psykologisk Institut, mimeo, 8 p.

Schiøler, P. (1987) *Paper at symposium*. University of Erasmus, Rotterdam. Jan. 1987, mimeo, 10 p.

Schutz A. (1971). *Collected Papers*. The Hague: Martinus Nihoff.

Schutz, A. (1974) *The structure of the life world*. London: Heinemann

Segal, B.M. (1986) The Soviet heavy drinking culture and the American heavy drinking subculture. In Babor, T. (ed.) *Alcohol and Culture*. New York: Annuals of the N.Y. Academy of Science, vol. 472.

Tulving, E. (1983). *Elements of episodic memory*. Oxford: Clarendon Press.

Websters Third New International Dictionary 1968.

2.

ALCOHOL CONSUMPTION
AND THE GROUPS OF SOCIETY

ALCOHOL CONSUMPTION
AND THE GROUPS OF SOCIETY

1. Introduction

At the Institute of Psychology, University of Aarhus, a major research project has been undertaken dealing with the 'Life of the Danes during the Crisis'. The project includes a survey of a representative Danish sample (2000 participants) in 1982, 1986 and 1988 (Petersen et al., 1987; Petersen et al., 1989).

In the 1988 survey opportunity was given to incorporate a few questions concerning alcohol and thus to couple the project of 'Alcohol Consumer Consciousness' (Sabroe, 1989) and the 'crisis project'. In one question was asked about the average amount of beer, wine, fortified wine and spirits drunk during a week, three questions concerned associations to the stimuli 'situations connected with beer' respectively 'wine and spirits', and two questions asked about 'reasons to drink' respectively 'reasons not to drink'. Only the primary results from the amount of consumption question will be dealt with in this article, cross tabulations and the analysis of the five remaining questions will be brought in a later article.

2. Alcohol consumption in general

In social science research the question of comparability is crucial. Regarding unities that constitute variables in social science, a single comparison can be drawn either between single unities - or especially at a macro level - between larger compounds of unities (systems).

When alcohol is the investigated variable one way could be - having a representative Danish material - to compare with other national representative data; another to split up the material into appropriate subgroups of the Danish society and compare these. In the present connection it is clearly the latter possibility which is relevant, and in the following alcohol consumption will be presented in relation to sex, age, social group, occupation, income, branches of trade and political affiliation. Irrespective of the focusing on 'internal comparison' it could be relevant to have a co-ordinated frame of reference besides the national (Danish). Briefly, it therefore shall be indicated at which level the Danish alcohol consumption is in a European perspective. The development of the quantitative consumption also shall be briefly indicated, especially with regard to the last decade. Two important things must be kept in mind about these official consumption figures, however. First, they are vitiated by errors when converted into average 'per capita' consumption, i.e. the average consumption of one person during a given period of time (normally the number of litre 100% alcohol per year/or centilitre per day). Second the figures represent very different patterns of consumption with subsequently different consequences for the alcohol users and their social surroundings in particular and the interpretation of national statistics in general.

After a very drastic fall in alcohol consumption in the beginning of this century, a period of more than 25 years showed a relatively stable consumption of 4-5 litre 100% alcohol pr. person beyond 14 years of age. But from the middle of the 1950'es and up to the middle of the 1970'es a rapidly increasing consumption up to 12 litre 100% alcohol per year per person beyond 14 years appeared. The period from the middle of the 1970'es up to the middle of the 1980'es showed a much shallower rise (an increase of 6-7%). The figures from the 1980'es, which are of interest to our investigation, show - disregarding an atypical 1983 - a relatively stable picture and in the last half of the 80'es there has been a decrease in the alcohol consumption (table 1). The figures are data from the so-called duty-corrected consumption, estimated by the Danish Department of Statistics.

Table 1: Alcohol consumption in Denmark 1980-90

YEAR	Litre 100% alcohol per inhabitant beyond 14 years of age
1980	11.7
1981	12.1
1982	12.4
1983	12.8
1984	12.2
1985	12.3
1986	12.1
1987	11.9
1988	11.6
1989	11.5
1990	11.5

A change in the composition of the consumption has taken place during the mentioned period. The consumption of wine has increased while the consumption of beer and to a lesser degree spirits has decreased. In the last half of the eighties the situation has been relatively stable with beer constituting approx. 60%, wine about 25% and spirits about 15% of the total consumption (source: Danish Dept. of Statistics).

In a Common Market perspective Denmark occupies a middle position regarding alcohol consumption, and in the frequent comparisons with the other Scandinavian countries - commonly regarded as constituting a common cultural background - Denmark clearly separates itself with a consumption twice as big as that of the other countries. But as already stated above, figures of consumption do not constitute an overall picture, regarding the important question of a relationship between level of national consumption and alcohol related problems no unique relationship is present, but apparently one finds a broad and general one (Thorsen, 1990).

3. Specific groupings of alcohol consumption

3.1. Method of data collection

In the survey six questions about alcohol were asked. In this article shall be dealt with only one of the questions. The question is worded: 'How many drinks on an average do you get per week of beer, wine, fortified wine and spirits?'. The use of the term 'drink' (in Danish: genstande) conforms to Danish practice, the term adopted as generally understandable and accepted describing the unit of one beer (33 cl), one glass of wine (12 cl) or one brandy or the like (3 cl), equivalent to 1.3 cl 100% alcohol.

In national as well as international alcohol research it is a well-known fact that far from all consumption is reported. In fact most often only half or less is reported. This problem shall not be discussed here, but regarding the wording of our question it is important to note that Sælan (1984) does not find significant differences in three different ways of asking questions, including questions about the average weekly consumption. For the National Institute of Social Research Körmendi (1986) has investigated the effect of using a telephone connecting between interviewer and interviewee. Nor were here substantial differences, although a tendency to state a larger consumption was seen in telephone interviews.

The investigation estimates the average consumption of adult Danes to be 6.69 drinks per week, with 3.23 being beer (48%), 2.34 wine (35%), 0.28 fortified wine (4%) and 0.84 spirits (13%). The discrepancy between these figures and the distribution issued from the National Statistical bureau is 10% less for beer and 10% higher for wine. Compared to other data on consumption the fact that more wine than beer is reported consumed in our investigation could result from the fact that the social/economic privileged groups in the investigated population are slightly overrepresented (cf. also article 3, p. 73). Converted to annual consumption in litres of 100% alcohol, which is the normal international scale, the consumption amounts to 4.52 litre. For 1987 the figures from the Danish department of Statistics are 11.6 litre 100% alcohol per year per person beyond 14 years. The figures in this article are calculated for the age group 16 years and up comparable with data from the earlier crisis investigations. The figures from the Danish Department of Statistics also include the 15-year-olds; thus 'beyond 14 years' which the Danish Department of Statistics use as table designation, means exclusive the 14-year-olds. The estimated consumption from the investigation is therefore a little too high as standard of reference for the figures from the Danish Dept. of Statistics, but compared to the official figures of consumption the underreporting amounts to at least 60%. The consumption stated in the investigation corresponds to what Körmendi (1986) registered.

3.2. The single variables

We have chosen to investigate sex, age, social group, income, occupation, trade and political affiliation. Clearly, the variables social group, income and occupation cannot be said to be independent of each other , nor can in the widest sense the three mentioned and sex and age. This situation will be discussed in article 3, at present the distribution of the single variables will be presented in their own right.

3.2.1. Sex

All international statistics show a considerable difference in the consumption among men and women. Registrations of a consumption for women of between one third and the half of men's are common. The consumption pattern has changed in the later years, however, and there has been an approximation, especially as regards the portion of the alcohol consumption which is wine.

Results of the total consumption show that one out of five Danes (20.5%) state that they don't drink alcohol. It is a surprisingly large figure compared with earlier statements about alcohol *abstainers*, showing normally 6-7%. Possibly, this large figure can be explained by the wording of the question. An analysis of the data and reports from the interviewers have shown that it obviously has been quite difficult for many interviewees to understand the conception 'average consumption per week', and it is the impression that many interviewees have in reality told how much they had consumed 'during the last week'. Compared to information regarding this type of consumption the figure is not surprising. Using the weekly consumption Sælan (1984) states 11.1% abstainers among his 40-year-olds, and Nielsen (1982) states that in her investigation 51% claimed not to have consumed alcohol the day before and 39% not to have consumed alcohol the previous week. In DIKE's (1987) investigation 27% state to have had no alcohol, neither the previous day nor the previous week-end. Apart from this, the distribution displays the usual picture. *A relatively small group (14%) drinks half of the total quantity of consumed alcohol, and those with a very small consumption (less than one drink a day) make up two thirds of the population.*

In table 2 the sex distribution in relation to numbers of drinks per week is stated for each of the four categories of alcohol.

Table 2: Number of drinks per week, sex distribution (percentage)

		Beer		Wine		Fort.Wine		Spirits		Total	
		M	F	M	F	M	F	M	F	M	F
0	drinks	20.5	52.7	38.2	41.0	83.4	84.8	56.6	76.0	12.7	28.2
1-6	drinks	53.0	44.0	53.3	53.7	16.1	14.6	38.8	22.8	36.4	48.6
7-13	drinks	16.4	2.8	7.0	4.0	0.5	0.7	3.8	1.1	28.2	17.9
14-20	drinks	6.7	0.3	0.6	0.7	-	-	0.7	0.1	12.2	3.6
21-	drinks	3.5	0.1	0.8	0.7	-	-	0.1	-	10.5	1.6
Average number of drinks		5.27	1.22	2.57	2.11	0.27	0.26	1.22	0.48	9.35	4.07

The table shows the average pattern for men and women for each of the four categories of alcohol. The uniformity of the picture in relation to wine and fortified wine clearly changes when looking upon beer and spirits, *placing men with a considerably higher consumption.* The difference is especially marked in relation to abstainers and those with a relatively large consumption. The total distribution of consumption is shown in table 3.

Table 3: Distribution of consumption on specific types of alcohol, men-women (percentage)

	Beer	Wine	Fort. wine	Spirits	Total
Men	81	55	50	72	70
Women	19	45	50	28	30
Total	48.1	35	4	13	100

The table repeats the information that the main difference lies in the consumption of beer, which at the same time accounts for half of the consumed alcohol, and to a lesser degree it applies to spirits, which only accounts for 1/8 of the consumption.

3.2.2 Age
In relation to age changes have taken place during the last decade with an earlier alcohol début as a result. But it has also been emphasized (Sælan, 1984) that especially the middle-aged have a considerable consumption. Table 4 shows the consumption distributed on age categories in 10 year divisions.

Table 4: Age-distribution of alcohol consumption (number of drinks per week)

	Below 20	20'es	30'es	40'es	50'es	Over 60	Total
Beer	3.20	3.27	3.57	3.74	3.07	2.42	3.23
Wine	1.48	1.92	2.83	3.55	2.14	1.40	2.34
Fort. wine	0.18	0.19	0.24	0.37	0.29	0.28	0.28
Spirits	0.96	0.85	0.52	0.81	0.93	1.17	0.84
Total	5.82	6.21	7.16	8.47	6.43	5.27	6.69

The distribution shows that *the 40-year-olds differ from the other groups with a significantly larger consumption* (5.72 litre 100% alcohol per year). At a yearly basis the 40-year-olds drink 1 litre 100% alcohol more than the 30-year-olds, who again drink 1/2 litre more than the 20- and 50-year-olds. The young below 20 years of age again drink half a litre less, and those above 60 state the smallest consumption with 3.56 litre 100% alcohol per year. It is especially the consumption of wine that accounts for the larger consumption among 40-year-olds. As for consumption of beer and fortified wine no large difference is found, and as for spirits the 40-year-olds are second lowest.

3.2.3 Social group
As shown in table 5 one finds a decreasing consumption of alcohol from social group 1 (highest) to social group 5 (lowest), the smallest consumption being in the rest group, however (i.e. those unplaceable in social group which is about 3% of the population). The division into social groups is the one used by the National Social Research Institute.

Table 5: Alcohol consumption with regard to social group (number of drinks per week)

	Soc.gr. 1	Soc.gr. 2	Soc.gr. 3	Soc.gr. 4	Soc.gr. 5	Rest-group	Total
Beer	3.80	3.22	3.40	3.34	3.10	1.14	3.23
Wine	5.08	4.02	3.01	1.89	1.20	0.54	2.34
Fort. wine	0.61	0.28	0.30	0.28	0.18	0.12	0.28
Spirits	1.79	1.05	0.82	0.75	0.77	0.37	0.84
Total	11.28	8.57	7.53	6.26	5.25	2.17	6.69

It is in the consumption of wine and spirits - and as regards social group 1 also fortified wine - that one finds the difference between the social groups.

3.2.4 Income
Looking at the respondents' gross income, the results show the same unequivocal distribution as for social group, and it is the consumption of wine here also- and to a certain degree spirits and beer - that separates the upper and lower groups on the scale of income (table 6).

Table 6:   Alcohol consumption according to own gross income (number of drinks per week)

	Low Income	Middle Income	High Income	No answer	Total
Beer	2.38	3.11	4.49	3.06	3.23
Wine	1.37	2.05	4.35	1.43	2.34
Fort. wine	0.20	0.27	0.38	0.20	0.27
Spirits	0.85	0.61	1.33	0.63	0.85
Total	4.80	6.04	10.55	5.32	6.69

As seen in the table, the high income group has a consumption 110% larger than that of the low income and 86% larger than that of the middle income group; the figures being very convincing thus.

3.2.5. Occupation
The investigation operates with 12 occupation groups. In order of precedence the result is shown in table 7.

Table 7: Alcohol consumption in relation to occupation (rank order/number of drinks per week)

	Beer	Wine	Fort. wine	Spirits	Total
Independent	5.61	3.34	0.47	0.90	10.30
Skilled worker	5.25	1.87	0.17	0.95	8.24
Employee/Civil servant	2.93	3.36	0.36	0.85	7.30
Student	3.61	1.82	0.08	1.01	6.52
Unemployed	3.06	1.96	0.23	0.72	5.96
Early retired	3.03	0.93	0.19	1.07	5.22
Unskilled worker	3.27	1.09	0.12	0.62	5.12
Pensioner	1.88	1.32	0.30	0.90	4.39
Helpmate	0.76	2.20	0.17	0.76	3.89
Farmer independent	2.42	0.79	0.12	0.38	3.72
House wife	1.00	0.66	0.18	0.61	2.45
Pupils	0.85	0.46	0.05	0.24	1.59
Total	3.23	2.34	0.28	0.84	6.69

In relation to the usual distribution picture it is remarkable that as for employees and civil servants (one third of the population) and for helpmates - which only accounts for 1% of the population - more wine than beer is consumed. With exception of the student group (8.5% of the population) - which is difficult to place on an occupation scale - the occupation distribution demonstrates that *the privileged in the labour market have the biggest alcohol consumption.* The weak groups in the labour market form a middle consumer group, and farmers and - as expected - the pure female groups (housewives and help mates) have the lowest consumption. Remarkable is also that *the independent* have a considerably larger consumption than even the closest following groups.

3.2.6 Branches of trade

The labour market can be divided in relation to trades also. Table 8 displays the order of precedence of alcohol consumption with regard to trades.

Table 8: Alcohol consumption in relation to branches of trade (rank order/number of drinks per week)

	Beer	Wine	Fort. wine	Spirits	Total
Building and con-struction	6.23	2.70	0.58	1.29	10.80
Commerce and res-taurant	3.86	3.56	0.30	1.15	8.87
Service	3.98	2.76	0.43	0.94	8.11
Industry and other forms of production	4.40	1.95	0.22	1.09	7.66
Public administration	2.93	2.46	0.29	0.72	6.40
Transport (private)	3.19	2.27	0.19	0.46	6.11
Education/culture	2.12	2.91	0.18	0.53	5.74
Public services (Post, train a.s.o.)	2.35	1.98	0.37	0.85	5.55
Defence and police	3.05	1.86	0.14	0.50	5.55
Social-/health sector	1.40	2.84	0.21	0.34	4.75
Agriculture	2.29	0.97	0.32	0.69	4.27

Employees in the 'building and construction sector' clearly differ from other trade groups as regards alcohol consumption, mostly because of a relatively large consumption of beer. The 'commerce and restaurant area', 'service', 'industry and other forms of production' henceforth compose a group with a comparingly high consumption, while 'agriculture' and the 'social and health sector' make up the low-consumption groups. Regarding the distribution on types of alcohol it is worthwhile to remark that the 'social-/health sector' and the 'education/culture sector' - the two groups with the lowest consumption of beer - are placed next and third highest with regard to wine consumption, and this wine consumption of the two groups is greater than for beer.

3.2.7 Political parties

An additional question to the biographical asked the respondents 'how they would cast their vote if there should be a general election to-morrow'. From this question derives the distribution of the amount of alcohol consumption shown in table 9, ranking the political parties according to the voters' average consumption.

Table 9: Political voting[1] and alcohol consumption (rank/amount of drinks per week)

	Beer	Wine	Fort. wine	Spirits	Total
Conservative (right wing)	2.90	3.31	0.47	1.13	7.81
Radical Left (liberal)	2.38	4.12	0.33	0.85	7.68
Socialist Peoples Party (left wing)	3.70	2.50	0.23	0.74	7.17
Progress Party (populist, right wing)	4.23	1.57	0.11	1.10	7.01
The Liberal Left (liberal, right wing)	2.43	2.42	0.39	0.95	6.15
Social Democrats (middle)	3.27	1.99	0.20	0.71	5.95
Centrum Democrats (liberal)	2.19	2.33	0.27	0.79	5.58
Christian Peoples Party(liberal)	0.68	0.57	0.29	0.18	1.72
Election abstainers	4.02	1.82	0.16	0.84	6.84
Total	3.23	2.34	0.28	0.84	6.69

---

1   The parties in 1988 were represented in the Danish Parliament with the following amount of seats: Social Democrats: 55, Conservative: 35, Socialist People's Party 24, The Liberal Left 22, Progress Party: 16, The Radical Left 10, Centrum Democrats: 9, The Christian People's Party: 4.

Parties, which in the representative population count less than 1% voters, are not included in the table. In all cases the parties in question are not represented in the Danish Parliament. The Christian-People's Party (liberal) differs from the other parties with a very low consumption of alcohol, but incidentally *voters of both the political wings are represented in as well the high as the low consumption end of the scale*. Results, which are worthwhile remarking, moreover are the Progress Party voter's (populist, right) - comparingly - high consumption of beer and the Radical Left voter's (liberal) high consumption of wine.

4. Summing up

The picture of the Danes' alcohol consumption presented in this article is not divergent from a picture drawn from investigations from the last decade (Nielsen, 1982; Sælan, 1984; DIKE, 1988). The picture given supplement with new data, and a few new angles, but the essential message is the consistency which is reflected across the involved variables. It is already mentioned that the variables are not mutually independent, but striking is nevertheless the *unambiguous picture of an increasing consumption of alcohol when one climbs up the social status ladder, an increasing consumption, when you are placed in the advantageous positions on the labour market, an increasing consumption when earnings are high*. It is men from these positions middle in life, who proportionally have the highest consumption of alcohol, and for these men consumption of wine plays a comparatively great role, as it does for the women of the same age from these groups. And all in all one can conclude that it seems as if high consumption of alcohol - at least in Denmark - does *not* represent a *poverty-culture* but *rather* is a sign of belongingness to a culture of affluence.

The attempt to relate alcohol consumption to the political spectrum did not give an unequivocal picture, it presented a couple of pronounced part-results, however.

5. Final remarks

In final comment I briefly shall return to the possibilities for further analysis of the data. It is obvious that one can continue with a cross-analysis with the demographical variables. This will take place in article 3. But an important possibility also is to investigate in relations between alcohol consumption and the socio-psychological variables used in the crisis project. The variables are:

I   Crisis consciousness
    a. Joint responsibility for the crisis
    b. External responsibility for the crisis
    c. Vision of the future
    d. Self-sacrifice

II   Experienced changes in life situation

III Psychological life-quality
    a. Personal thriving
    b. Thriving in society
    c. Stress

IV   Resources of acting
    a. Offensive action
    b. Adaptive resignation

V   Changes in style of life

VI   Attitudes
    a. attitude to work
    b. attitude to unemployment
    c. attitude to the role of the state.

A first and rough analysis seems to indicate that there is only a few significant relations between these variables and the amount of consumption of alcohol, but a couple of important ones, however: The greater the adaptive resignation the less consumed alcohol, and the more oriented towards an ecological style of life the less consumed alcohol. But a preliminary impression must be that individual psychological variables - at least as they are defined in the crisis project - has little connection with alcohol consumption. It is the socially important aspects of person characteristics and the social determined aspects of life which are important, factors of which the latter also is important in the constitution of the Alcohol Consumer Consciousness.

References

Alkohol og Narkotikarådet (1988) *Alkohol og Narkotikamisbruget 1987.* København: Alkohol- og Narkotikarådets skriftserie 13. (Alcohol and Drug Misuse), 1987)

DIKE (Dansk Institut for Klinisk Epidemiologi) (1988): *Sundhed og sygelighed i Danmark, 1987.* København: DIKE. (Health and illness in Denmark, 1987).

Körmendi, E. (1986) *Datakvalitet ved telefoninterview.* København: Socialforskningsinstituttet, studie 52. (Quality of data in telephone interviews)

Nielsen, Kirsten (1982) *Danskernes Alkoholvaner.* København: Alkohol og Narkotikarådet. (Alcohol habits of the Danes)

Petersen, E., Sabroe, K-E., Kristensen, O.S., Sommerlund, B. (1987) *Danskernes tilværelse under krisen I-II.* Aarhus: Aarhus Universitetsforlag (The Danes during the Crisis). (The thriving of Danes during the crisis I-II)

Petersen, E., Andersen, J.G., Dahlberg, J., Sabroe, K-E., Kristensen, O.S., Sommerlund, B. (1987) *The Conscious and self-sacrificing Danes.* Aarhus: Institute of Psychology, press.

Sabroe, K.-E. (1989). Alcohol Consumer Consciousness. A social psychological perspective on alcohol. In: *35th ICCA Proceedings, vol. IV,* 1-21. Oslo: National Directorate for the Prevention of Alcohol and Drug Dependence.

Sælan, H. (1984) *Alkohol og alkoholisme.* København: FADL's forlag. (Alcohol and alcoholism)

Thorsen, T. (1990). *Hundrede års alkoholmisbrug.* København: Alkohol- og Narkotikarådet. (Hundred years alcohol abuse)

3.

SOCIAL GROUP PATTERNS
AND ALCOHOL CONSUMPTION

SOCIAL GROUP PATTERNS
AND ALCOHOL CONSUMPTION

1. Social consciousness

In article 2 was presented a first analysis of the alcohol related data from a large survey on the crisis behaviour of the Danes. The results were explained through a consumer analysis related to the groupings of society. The picture that could be based on this analysis naturally had to appear as a broad and relatively rough description. But a so prominent consistency appeared, through the different sets of data, that one could formulate a very clear assumption saying that a relatively high level of alcohol consumption in Denmark (seen in a society group perspective) is not an indication of a "poverty culture", but is connected with the part of the public who have a social and financial surplus - who relatively seen are "the rich ones" (Sabroe, 1986).

The goal of a continued analysis is to make this rough picture more detailed. Two sets of analyses will be carried out in following up on this. In the present article a number of relevant two-sided analyses will be undertaken with point of departure in the applied biographical and social variables and in the average consumption per week. In a following article a special group - the heavy drinkers - will be taken up, and attempts will be undertaken to characterize this consumption group through the applied biographical and social variables.

Apart from the fundamental reason of a general expansion of our knowledge, the motivation for the undertaking of a deeper analysis is to secure as solid a foundation as possible for launching prevention initiatives. It is evident that the ultimate goal for a prevention effort must be the individual person. Through acquisition of knowledge of how alcohol appears as a subject in society, the individual person establishes the prerequisite to reflect on this presence - its possibilities, limitations, consequences etc. - that is the individual could be more alcohol consumption conscious (Sabroe, 1989a). Coupled with individual resources in the broadest sense this leads to concrete action possibilities, in which the basis of action is a knowledge-founded freedom of action and a responsibility of action. A placement of alcohol in life quality connection must always have its basis in these two last-mentioned conditions.

The existence of alcohol in society and the possibility with relatively few restrictions to be able to drink alcohol more or less when convenient, is an objective characteristic of the social reality in Denmark. The individual acquires this condition, and through a subjective processing it obtains a special character and causes special action incitements. But it is evident that the individual is not isolated in its being and behaviour; he/she joins different social groupings and can be influenced by common behaviour patterns in these groups. Fundamentally, it is important to remember that the effect of alcohol depends on the following three-sided fact: the chemical characteristics of alcohol, the characteristics of the individual person and the social circumstances under which alcohol is consumed. Simultaneously, it is also important to remember that alcohol cannot be regarded as an isolated phenomenon in social life; it is a cultural phenomenon and as such is subject to the cultural ruptures that occur in the historical development. Alcohol, however, has from time immemorial been a central means of establishing the state of changed consciousness called inebriation, and the phenomenon of inebriation has always been one of the most difficult for society to "subdue", and it still is in the present society. But much indicates that mankind is split up regarding the taming of the search for intoxication. Consumption figures show that apparently women have been "more effective", or maybe they apply other means to enter a state of altered consciousness.

Another important relation to take into consideration is that the individual's consumption of alcohol shows a relative stability over time or, statistically stated as an invariance over periods of time, and that the same condition applies to the different sub-populations within a cultural/national entity (Sabroe, 1989b). In a developmental perspective this seems to call for an understanding, which must be based on the fact that socially specific interaction processes are the fundamentals of drinking behaviour, that the different conditions being a part of this do not occur as isolated phenomena, but that they are multiplicative in their effect, and that changes in drinking behaviour can be seen as proportional to the initial drinking behaviour. Points of view alike have been stated by Skog (1980, 1985), and Lemmens (1990) has been dealing with the problem also.

Sabroe (1989a, and article one) argues in favour of a frame of understanding of alcohol-related behaviour based on the individual-oriented concept of Alcohol

Consumer Consciousness, and a preliminary definition of the concept is suggested. A short, supplementing presentation can be found in article four in this book. But referring to the analyses to be brought in the present article it could be relevant to mention the sociologically oriented concept "the social consciousness". Durkheim's concept, collective consciousness (1972, 1978, orig. 1895, 1897), is an early and central attempt in European sociology to delimit this conception. In his determination of social consciousness, he saw the basis for an understanding of society. Society cannot be explained through the individual, but the individual is a conditional element for the existence of a society. However, the individual is "subjected" to a system of interacting phenomena (common attitudes, values, etc.) - the collective consciousness. The collective consciousness has a life beyond the individual, it continues even when the individuals have disappeared who at a given time constitute a given society or a social group (cit. Sabroe, 1984, p. 59).

In the present connection, social consciousness will be understood as cognitions (knowledge, attitudes, convictions, feelings, action incitements, etc.) that are shared by a number of individuals. The individuals are aware (or could be made aware) of their mutual possessions of the cognitions. The cognitions are tied up with subject areas, and the consequences can be observed in the actions of the individual. But how the cognitions are rooted is not necessarily fully in the awareness of the individual and not necessarily immediately revocable.

The social consciousness is formed not only by a casual knowledge but includes cognitions which are bound to (practical) everyday activities in the group that shares the social consciousness from linguistic forms of expression to material and immaterial products of culture. Social consciousness is an individually acquired but mutually accepted basis for actions (establishing of goals for action and methods for obtaining these goals) that across and possibly independently of the individual's own immediate interests leads to the fulfilment of common social demands. However, the individual is not lost in this "commonness". By and large every individual has a field which can be defined as the sphere of influence within which he or she has got the possibility of influencing other people or social groups, through his/her being and knowledge.

Alcohol has a particular value and special place in Danish culture, but there are subcultural values which emphasize the possible individual behaviour in a social connection. The consequences of such values to the individual or group can be of great importance and therefore should be considered when planning prevention initiatives. Though, being on a relatively general level signals about values sent out by such groupings can, as a first step, be identified through thorough descriptions of the consumer behaviour in (relevant) groupings, as it will be done in the following.

In the considerations stated so far a picture based on knowledge and responsibility as always existing possibilities has been drawn, and the picture is used mainly the light shades of the colour spectrum. But this is just a partial picture. To reach a total depiction also the dark shades have to be considered. It is evident that alcohol can ruin life-quality and life together, when it is abused. It is evident that large economical resources are tied up in society's effort to fight the alcohol-related problems. But it is also evident that we speak of a processual course, when the consumption of alcohol becomes problematic (Elmeland, Nygaard & Sabroe, 1990). It is important, therefore, to be able to understand the general social basis from which this process starts. "The ordinary consumption" must always be the foundation from which abuse is evaluated, and on which a rational prevention action must be based. A contribution to this understanding are the facts put forward below. In a following article (chapter 4) the consciousness problem will be elaborated, and the heavy consumer of alcohol will be target of the analyses. In the following sections there will be brought a number of cohesion-analyses in which the previously presented background variables (Sabroe, 1989b) will be examined in their interactions. I have chosen to bring these two-sided analyses, and not to use more extensive multivariate analyses, on the assumption that a relatively unambiguous picture will be the result of the "simple" two-sided analysis. With the applied variables 21 two-sided cross tabulations would be possible. Not all of them will be presented, however; a number of couplings between for example trade, political affiliation, income and other variables are found not to be relevant from a psycho- or sociological point of view.

2. Sex and consumption in relation to age, social group, income, trace and political affiliations

2.1. Sex and age

The tendency, found for the total population, that the consumption is highest among the 40-year-olds also applies for both of the sexes (table 1).

Table 1:   Average consumption per week in relation to sex and age

Sex	<20	20'ies	30'ies	40'ies	50'ies	>60	Total
Men	8.50	8.95	10.08	12.11	9.54	6.78	9.35
Women	3.68	3.67	4.66	5.09	3.26	3.29	4.07
Total	5.82	6.21	7.16	8.47	6.43	5.27	6.69
Ratio	2.3/1	2.4/1	2.2/1	2.4/1	2.9/1	2.1/1	2.3/1
p = .000							

With a slightly greater difference in the second eldest age group there is - surprisingly - approximately the same ratio between men and women across the age groups. It is surprising also that in the age group above 60 women have a relatively high consumption compared to men. Maybe this is an expression of the idea that "a drink before bedtime" as a substitute for sleeping pills has caught on.

2.2. Sex and social group

The results shown in table 2 gives an unambiguous picture of a difference between men's and women's consumption in all social groups, with women consuming the lowest amount.

Table 2: Average consumption per week in relation to sex and social group

Sex	Social group						
	1	2	3	4	5	Rest gr.	Total
Men	11.86	9.99	9.28	8.62	9.29	4.86	9.35
Women	9.40	6.35	5.24	3.97	2.79	1.80	4.07
Total	11.28	8.57	7.53	6.26	5.25	2.17	6.69
Ratio	1.3/1	1.6/1	1.8/1	2.2/1	3.3/1	2.7/1	2.3/1
p = .000							

There is a clear difference among the social groups concerning the consumption ratio for men and women, however, with a relation between the sexes which approaches 1 to 1 for social group 1, whereas it is more than 3 to 1 for social group 5. The difference between men's and women's consumption is growing moreover when going from social group 1 to 5. The rest group is a relatively small number of persons, who were impossible to place in a social group.

2.3 Sex and income

For the income groups a picture appears indicating that men as well as women report a higher consumption with a growing income (table 3). But there are clear differences among the income groups regarding the relative share of men's and women's consumption.

Table 3: Average consumption per week in relation to sex and income

Sex	Low	Middle	High	Total
Man	7.65	8.30	11.09	9.35
Woman	3.32	4.17	8.19	4.07
Total	4.80	6.04	10.55	6.69
Ratio	2.3/1	2.0/1	1.3/1	2.3/1
$p = .0000$				

In the high-income group, men and women have almost the same consumption (the ratio: 1.3 to 1), while the men in the low-income group have more than double the consumption in relation to the women.

2.4 Sex and trade

In no trades the women even come near the men regarding amount of alcohol consumed (table 4). Closest are men and women among the young groups of students and pupils, and among employees and civil servants. But even here the consumption among men is almost twice as high as for women.

In the opposite end we find unemployed and pensioners, in which groups the men's consumption is four times as high as the women's.

Table 4:   Average consumption per week in relation to sex and trade

Trade	Sex		Total	Ratio
	Men	Women		
Student	8.28	4.79	6.52	1.7/1
Employee/civil servant	9.82	5.43	7.30	1.8/1
Pupil, apprentice	4.92	2.71	1.59	1.8/1
Independent	11.89	4.72	10.30	2.5/1
Skilled worker	10.26	3.80	8.24	2.7/1
Early retired	7.84	2.89	5.22	2.8/1
Unskilled worker	8.89	2.59	5.12	3.4/1
Unemployed	11.42	2.80	5.96	4.1/1
Pensioner	8.47	2.04	4.39	4.2/1
Farmer	3.87	.0	3.72	-
Helpmate	.0	3.91	3.89	-
Housewife	.0	2.72	2.45	-
Total	9.35	4.07	6.69	2.3/1
$p = .000$				

If the two columns are placed in rank order interesting differences appear (figure 1). In some groups there are little difference between the placing of men and women, but four trades show important differences in the order of appearance. Women are ranking highest among employees/civil servants, the men being number four. Women studying are in a second place, the male students ranking number seven. In the opposite end unskilled women are number ten while the men rank number five. The unemployed women are relatively low in rank (number seven) but the unemployed lie second highest and together with independent men differ significantly from the others.

Figure 1: Order of rank sex - trade (number of drink per week)

Men	Women
1 Independent	1 Employee/civil servant
2 Unemployed	2 Student
3 Skilled worker	3 Independent
4 Employee/civil servant	4 Helpmate
5 Unskilled worker	5 Skilled worker
6 Pensioner	6 Early retired
7 Student	7 Unemployed
8 Early retired	8 Housewife
9 Pupil, apprentice	9 Pupil, apprentice
10 Farmer	10 Unskilled worker
	11 Pensioner

In terms of trade, the unemployed women in the population of the investigation constitute the relatively largest group compared to the men, being almost twice as many as the unemployed men. Related to their recorded low consumption one here finds an explanation of the relatively low total consumption for which the unemployed account in a total-population connection (Sabroe, 1989b), a result that has been disputed somewhat.

2.5 Sex and political affiliation

The relationship between men's and women's consumption proves that - when the difficultly placeable parties: "The Progress Party" and "The Christian People's Party" are left out - one finds a greater similarity in consumption between women and men in the right wing and liberal parties than among Social Democrats and Social People's Party (left wing) (table 5). It is remarkable, though, that men from the Social People's Party report the highest consumption and the women are in a third place.

Table 5: Average consumption per week in relation to sex and political affiliation[1]

Political party	Men	Women	Total	Ratio
Social Democrats	9.40	3.75	5.95	2.5/1
Christian People's Party	2.80	1.11	1.71	2.5/1
Progress Party	10.25	4.11	7.01	2.5/1
Social People's Party	10.55	4.84	7.17	2.2/1
The Liberal Left	7.82	3.83	6.15	2.0/1
The Centre Democrats	6.93	3.70	5.58	1.9/
Radical Left	10.03	5.47	7.68	1.8/1
Conservative	9.72	5.50	7.86	1.8/1
Total	9.35	4.07	6.69	2.3/1
p = .000				

1) For position of parties and numbers in the Danish Parliament, see article 2, p. 43.

3. Age and consumption in relation to income, social group, and political affiliation

3.1. Age and income

Apart from the two youngest groups, in which only relatively few are in the high-income group, there is an unambiguous picture across the age groups with a growing consumption when we go from the low-income group to the high-income group (table 6). It proves that for all groups, apart from the group under 20 years of age - in which is registered only one person out of 115 with a high income - the high-income group has the highest consumption. In the low-income group and the middle-income group it is the 40-year-olds who have the highest average consumption, while in the high-income group it is the 50- and 60-years old.

Table 6:   Average consumption per week in relation to age and income

Age	Income			
	Low	Middle	High	Total
<20	5.22	7.63	4.00	5.82
20'ies	6.04	5.21	9.61	6.21
30'ies	5.98	6.11	10.14	7.16
40'ies	6.26	7.23	10.85	8.47
50'ies	3.49	5.91	10.97	6.43
>60	3.96	5.76	11.83	5.27
Total	4.80	6.04	10.55	6.69
p = .000				

3.2. Age and social group

The youngest age group differs from the rest in not being represented in social group 1 and by the fact that 98% are placed in social group 4 and 5. With exception from this group the highest average consumption across the age groups exists in social group 1 and 2, as shown in table 7.

Table 7:   Average consumption per week in relation to age and social group

Age	Social group						
						Rest group	Total
	1	2	3	4	5		
<20	.0	6.00	13.67	6.60	5.49	.0	5.82
20'ies	11.67	7.23	6.43	6.88	4.30	0.67	6.21
30'ies	9.12	7.19	8.03	6.41	6.43	0.67	7.16
40'ies	11.13	11.32	9.21	7.55	6.06	3.33	8.47
50'ies	12.64	9.12	6.92	6.11	5.22	1.19	6.34
>60	13.67	8.05	6.34	4.08	4.32	2.84	5.27
Total	11.28	8.57	7.53	6.26	5.25	2.17	6.69
p = .000							

On average, the 40-years old in social group 1 consume slightly less than those in group 2, but otherwise there is across the age groups a declining consumption from social group 1 to 5. The oldest of age (>60) from social group 1 have the highest average consumption, when the analysis is being based on age and social group.

3.3 Age and political affiliation

The representative consumption figures show that the highest consumption lies with the 40- (and 30-) year-olds (cf. article 2). But examining the connection age and political affiliation in relation to consumption the picture changes for several political groupings.

In table 8, the connection between "large-scale" consumption, age and political affiliation is illustrated. In order to give a better illustration a graphic layout is used instead of figures. The table is designed in a way that reflects the age groups which have the highest average consumption. The choice has been to mark out the two highest placed age groups, or, if there is only little difference between these, the three highest placed groups. In most of the cases there will be a clear difference in the average consumption between these groups and the following, and the differences within and among the political parties are highly significant. The data show a picture of great differences among the parties, but there are no ready explanations on the distribution which does not follow a usual pattern, especially concerning the placing of the Liberal Left Party and the Radical Left.

Table 8: Average consumption per week in relation to age and political affiliation

Political Party	<20	20'ies	30'ies	40'ies	50'ies	>60
The Liberal Left[1]		|-----------------|				
The Radical Left[2]		|---------------------------|				
Social People's Party[3]	|--------|		|-------|		|-------|	
The Centre Democrats[4]			|------------------|			
Social Democrats[5]				|-----------------|		
Christian People's Party[6]				|-----------------|		
The Progress Party[7]			|-------|		|-------|	
Conservative[8]					|-----------------|	
AVERAGE			|-----------------|			

Positions: 1) Liberal, right; 2) Liberal; 3) Left; 4) Liberal; 5) Centre; 6) Liberal; 7) Populist right; 8) Right

It should be noticed that the age-based distribution between the political parties does not seem to contribute to an explanation of the difference in age-based consumption. Among other things the age distribution in table 9 shows that the four old parties in Danish politics (Social Democrats, Radical Left, Conservatives, and the Left Party) have a profile of 16-19% in the youngest age group, but with a varying weight of middle-aged and older people, while Social People's Party is based mostly on the young ones (with 30%) and first adult years. The Progress Party is well represented among the youngest also, but otherwise has an even distribution across the age groups. These profiles have no evident connection to the clear difference in the distributions of consumption, which call for explanation through other variables.

Table 9:   Age spread in relation to party (%)

Party[1]	<20	20'ies	30'ies	40'ies	50'ies	>60	
Social Democrats	4	15	23	19	16	22	100%
Radical Left	1	16	27	32	11	12	100%
Conservative	4	12	24	20	18	22	100%
Social People's Party	5	25	41	16	7	6	100%
Christian People's Party	0	4	28	14	18	36	100%
The Liberal Left	4	13	11	18	27	27	100%
The Progress Party	4	23	18	19	17	19	100%

1) Positions in parliament (Folketing), see table 8.

4. Political affiliation

4.1. Political affiliation and social group

The social group membership proves to be a dominant factor across the political parties (table 10). It applies to all parties that social group 1, except for the Progress Party (and Christian People's Party where it does not exist) has the highest consumption. It applies to the five parties: Social Democrats, Radical Left, Conservative, Centre Democrats and the Left Party furthermore, that there is a gradually declining consumption from social group 1 to social group 5. Social People's Party (and Christian People's Party with fairly small figures, however) differ from this pattern with a relatively high consumption in social group 4 and 5. The Progress Party shows a picture opposite to the dominating with the highest consumption in social group 5 and a declining consumption towards group 1.

Table 10: Average consumption per week in relation to social group and party

Party	Social Group					
	1	2	3	4	5	Average
Conservative	11.6	11.2	9.3	4.3	4.1	7.81
The Centre Democrats	11.5	8.6	6.8	4.0	2.5	5.58
The Liberal Left	11.1	7.1	7.1	5.8	4.3	6.15
Social Democrats	10.8	8.9	8.8	6.2	5.2	5.95
Radical Left	10.5	9.3	8.8	7.0	1.3	7.68
Social People's Party	9.7	7.9	5.2	8.1	7.0	7.17
The Progress Party	3.0	6.7	6.2	7.8	9.6	7.01
Christian People's Party	.0	1.7	0.2	4.0	2.4	1.71
TOTAL	11.28	8.57	7.53	6.26	5.25	6.69
p = .0000						

4.2. Political affiliation and income

In table 11 one finds a clearly higher consumption in the high-income group across all of the political parties. For all parties except for Social People's Party and Christian People's Party there is also a distinctive fall in the average consumption, when going from high over middle to low incomes. As it was the case in the cross tabulation including social group, three parties (the same) differ from the general pattern. For Social People's Party, The Progress Party, and Christian People's Party there is a clearly smaller difference between the consumption in the high- and low-income groups, and for Social People's Party (and Christian People's Party) the second highest consumption is found in the low-income group. With an expected connection between income and social group placing, the results are not surprising.

Table 11: Average consumption per week in relation to income and political party

Political Party	Income			Average
	High	Middle	Low	
Radical Left	11.7	6.1	2.5	7.68
The Left Party	11.2	5.8	2.5	6.15
Conservative	10.7	7.5	4.6	7.81
Social Democrats	10.5	6.3	5.1	5.95
Social People's Party	9.7	6.4	7.6	7.17
The Progress Party	8.8	6.6	5.8	7.01
The Centre Democrats	8.6	5.1	2.2	5.58
Christian People's Party	1.3	1.9	1.5	1.71
AVERAGE	10.55	4.80	6.04	6.69
p = .0000				

4.3. Political affiliation and trade

The table serving as a basis for the analysis is relatively hard to grasp with its ten times eight entries. The figures shown in brackets in table 12 furthermore are based on a small number of persons (>5) and should be interpreted carefully in the analysis.

Table 12: Average consumption per week in relation to political party and trade

	Political Party								
	A	B	C	SF	CD	Q	V	Z	Average
Independent	22.3	(13.3)	12.8	(1.0)	(4.0)	-	9.2	5.9	10.3
Skilled worker	8.1	7.3	6.4	10.0	(3.8)	-	(8.3)	11.9	8.24
Employee/ Civil servant	6.9	9.6	9.0	6.9	7.7	2.1	7.7	5.7	7.30
Student	6.3	3.3	6.1	7.3	-	-	4.2	9.0	6.52
Unemployed	3.4	(2.3)	(2.7)	4.4	-	-	(11.8)	(6.4)	5.96
Early retired	4.4	3.0	(4.5)	4.2	6.6	(1.8)	4.6	12.7	5.22
Unskilled worker	5.9	(0.5)	3.1	6.3	(6.0)	(0.5)	8.0	5.6	5.12
Pensioner	4.8	-	4.4	(24.3)	2.7	-	(4.0)	(11.1)	4.39
Helpmate	-	(6.0)	(4.6)	-	(1.0)	(.0)	2.0	(12.0)	3.89
Farmer	-	-	(8.0)	-	(4.0)	-	3.1	3.9	3.72
Housewife	(6.1)	(0.5)	3.6	(2.0)	(0.5)	(0.5)	(1.0)	(0.5)	2.45
Pupil/apprentice	(6.3)	-	(1.3)	(4.5)	-	-	-	-	1.59
	5.95	7.68	7.81	7.17	5.58	1.72	6.15	7.01	6.69

p = .0000

A: Social Democrats (centre)
B: Radical Left (liberal)
C: Conservative (right)
SF: Social People's Party (left)
CD: The Centre Democrats (liberal)
Q: Christian People's Party (liberal)
V: The Liberal Left (liberal, right)
Z: The Progress Party (populist, right)

But the most conspicuous thing is that the independent in the four old parties in Danish Politics (A, B, C and V) form the group with the highest average consumption, and this differs significantly from the average consumption of the other groups. Noticeably also is that the independent in the Progress Party differ from the independent in the other political parties with a clearly lower average consumption, whereas The Progress Party's group of voters of "early retired" have a clearly higher average consumption than those of the other political parties.

5. Summing up and discussion

In connection with preventive efforts, an important information could be knowl-edge of the general patterns of the alcohol consumption in society. Apart from the fact that the goal of prevention efforts is individual behaviour, it must be considered that alcohol behaviour is "embedded" in social connections. The indi-vidual is together with others in most of his or her alcohol consumption, often being in primary groups. This consumption behaviour can be controlled by spe-cific sets of small group norms, but also more general sets of tendencies applying to fairly large groupings or to society as an entity. In the analyses presented in the parts 2, 3 and 4 a picture has been drawn which clearly shows that across all social groups men consume more alcohol than women. Among the groupings a fairly varied pattern exists, the groupings also show general tendencies on the other hand.

Across sex it is the 40-year-olds who have the highest average consumption, but the consumption ratio of men and women in the different age groups displays great similarity. If social group is chosen as a criterion one finds, on the other hand, clear differences; the higher the social group, the more alike in their con-sumption are men and women. The same applies to income. For both sex the consumption is highest in the high-income group, and the higher the income the more alike in their alcohol consumption are men and women. If political affilia-tion is chosen as criterion, a greater equality in men's and women's consumption is found among the right wing and liberal parties than among Social Democrats and Social Peoples Party.

With age as basis, it can be determined in the same way that it is the high-income groups who have the highest consumption across the ages, and, equally, it is the upper social groups. A picture then is drawn which further emphasizes the im-pression from the general consumer analyses (Sabroe, 1989b). It proves that the highest consumption is registered in the highly placed groupings in society, ir-respective of sex and age. Supplementary analyses regarding trade and political affiliation support this picture.

A fact appearing from this analysis is the extent which the alcohol consumption assumes among women in the upper social groupings. We know that the average consumption is highest in these groups, and when the ratio for men and women gets as close as 1.3/1, we may find cause to "call to arms". At least if we take a starting point in the dominating assumption that women belong in the low-consumption groups, or, as it has been maintained in Holmila (1988) that women traditionally are thought of as a controlling agent regarding men's (husbands, co-habitants) drinking, that is as a potentially "preventing factor" in relation to a large male consumption. With the ratio of 1.3/1 there is a similar situation for men and women in the upper social groups concerning the influence of alcohol (per thousand in the blood). The similarity in social behaviour and the common experience situations, which characterize the relatively more affluent groups in society seems to have - as a "consequence of equality" - a high and with regard to effect a homogeneous alcohol consumption. For women, to a higher degree than for men, the education factor seems to be of importance for a high ranking on the consumption scale, a circumstance that could be worthwhile considering in connection with a prevention initiative.

References

Durkheim, E. (1895/1972). *Den sociologiske metode.* København: Gyldendal. (The sociological method)

Durkheim, E. (1897/1978). *Selvmordet.* København: Fremad. (The suicide)

Holmila, Marja (1988). *Wives, husbands and alcohol. A study of informal drinking control within the families.* Helsinki: Finnish Foundation for Alcohol Studies, vol. 36.

Lemmens, P.H.H.M. (1990). *Measurement and distribution of alcohol consumption.* Maastricht: Krips Repro Meppel.

Petersen, E., Andersen, J.G., Dahlberg-Larsen, J., Sabroe, K.-E. & Sommerlund, B. (1989). *De krisebevidste og offervillige danskere.* Aarhus: Psykologisk Institut. (The crisis-conscious and self-sacrificing Danes)

Rasmussen, O. & Sabroe, K.-E. (1989). *Danskernes Alkohol Forbruger Bevidsthed. Frekvensanalyser.* Aarhus: Psykologisk Institut. (The Danes' Alcohol Consumer Consciousness. Frequency analysis)

Sabroe, K.-E. (1984). *Socialpsykologi.* Copenhagen: Akademisk Forlag. (Social psychology)

Sabroe, K.-E. (1989a). Alcohol consumer consciousness. A social psychological perspective on alcohol. In *Proceedings ICAA, vol. IV,* 1-21. Oslo: National Directorate for the Prevention of Alcohol and Drug Problems.

Sabroe, K.-E. (1989b). Alkohol og samfundets grupperinger. In E. Petersen et al. *De krisebevidste og offervillige danskere.* Aarhus: Psykologisk Institut. (Alcohol and the groupings of society)

Skog, O.J. (1980). Social issues and the distribution of alcohol consumption. *Journ. Drug Issues, 10,* 71-92.

Skog, O.J. (1985). The collectivity of drinking cultures: a theory of distribution of alcohol consumption. *Brit.Journ.Addict, 80*, 83-99.

4.

HEAVY CONSUMPTION OF ALCOHOL
AND SOCIAL GROUPINGS

HEAVY CONSUMPTION OF ALCOHOL AND SOCIAL GROUPINGS

1. Alcohol and consciousness

In Sabroe (1989), consciousness is characterized as the individual's possibility for actively and anticipating/reflecting to be able to relate to his/her possibility of acting. It was pointed out also that to have a covering picture of the individual's possibilities, these had to be seen as rooted in society. In the course of life the individual is met by social conditions that can be designated as the objective foundation for acting. This potential foundation of acting is confronted by the individual's subjectively motivated interests of life. The outcome of this encounter will reflect the individual's processing of his/her life-situation, it will indicate the amount of control the individual has obtained and the potentiality for establishing changes of the life situation. Experiences of quality of life will also be determined by this interplay (cf. also article 1).

To react actively conscious - in the meaning just stated - is always a prospect of acting for the individual. But, if a conscious conducting oneself in the actual life-situation will take place, will be a matter of the relationship between the prospects/restrictions actually and objectively set and the subjective reasons for acting which is a result of previous processing of individual life conditions.

When the individual acts during daily-life it is clearly subjectively motivated, and the acts originate in the life-interest of the individual. But the acts do not take place "in isolation", own interests and common interests tied up with primary and secondary groupings will always jointly be present as a foundation for acting.

Alcohol is a societal subject in relation to which subjective reasons for acting will be present, and in relation to which ambivalent sets of signals exist. But a prevailing signal has had, in the later years, the message: Reduce alcohol consumption. This signal is transmitted as a universal message and is presented in the media, in general. But the target of the signal is the single human being. If the individual is the ultimate target, it is the individual's general and specific experiences with relation to alcohol which should be the foundation for research aimed at prevention, not as it often has been the case the societal damaging consequences. To understand the substance: alcohol, one must understand alcohol as a general subject for the individuals in their existence in the culture in question, but also the specific reasons which is characteristic for the single individuals in relating to the substance alcohol.

A complete understanding cannot be based on cultural-historic or individual-historic conditions alone, however. They establish frames in their joint activity and the conscious-oriented consequences hereof with necessity must be uncovered. But the attributes of the substance alcohol must be incorporated, attributes which acutely have general and specific effects on the central nervous system and through a continued heavy-use have damaging influence on somatic conditions. These perspectives are outside what can be taken up in this article though. The object is a description of a population based on consumption and demographic data.

2. Heavy consumption of alcohol

2.1. Reasons for heavy consumption

As is the case for many other problems of human behaviour, explanations of heavy drinking have been put forward drawing on frames of understanding from biology, individual psychology, social psychology, and social science. In the present context such considerations will not be presented, but regarding the demarcation of the heavy-user group the biological and social science approach have been dominating. Central is the point of view from the later years, however, that no "grand theory" has been established, and that different factors presumably have to be brought in when explaining consumption at different social strata and for different levels of consumption, for example "normal" consumption in relation to "extensive/harmful" consumption.

Two major orientations have been in the front within the last four or five decades concerning consumption characterized as abuse . In one tradition the term "alcoholism" was adopted as the designation for a disease-related condition. The term was officially taken over by WHO (1952) and was defined: "Alcoholics are those excessive drinkers whose dependence on alcohol has attained such a degree that it shows a noticeable mental disturbance or an interference with their bodily and mental health, their inter-personal relations, and their smooth social and economic functioning; or who show the prodromal signs of such developments."

A second tradition has questioned the appropriate in placing alcohol-dependency within a disease understanding. This point of view is maintained even confronted with the results of twin research and biological research, from which it is claimed that hereditary or congenital factors seems to be decisive in developing an alcohol-dependency. The critic obtained considerable influence in WHO, and in 1979 the term "alcoholism" was deleted from the International Classification of Disease and replaced by the concept "Alcohol Dependence Syndrome".

Prior to this replacement, a task group had been working ending up with the book: "Alcohol related disabilities" (Edwards et al., 1977). The message from the task group was that the etiology of alcohol abuse could be understood when including a broad pattern of interacting psychological and social conditions, only, coupled with alcohol's concrete, physical damaging effects. From this point of view the consequences of abuse is brought beyond an individual condition of health (somatic, psychic or social) and is supplemented with a relation-perspective which is important not the least when considering preventive activities.

2.2 Prevention of heavy drinking

Alcohol abuse cannot be regarded as an isolated phenomenon/problem easily remedied through more control and restrictions. Alcohol abuse is one of several possible "answers" to community-created conditions of functioning and the individual's relating to these conditions. Therefore, an analysis ought to uncover the societal, economical and political circumstances that establish the scope of actions, which objectively are available with regard to alcohol. At which level of reality is alcohol present, how is the general concept of alcohol experienced by the individual, by which symbolism is alcohol present in the social interplay?

In this connection questions could be raised if heavy consumption of alcohol is a symptomatic consequence of a given life-situation? Or does a heavy consumption represent a conscious relating to the life conditions of the heavy user? Has the heavy user acknowledged her/his potentials of acting? Has she/he learned to manage these, learned to take a stand? If this is the case, why has the choice been heavy-consumption? Has the relationship between the immediate life-expansion as heavy-consumer and the attitudes from society to this existence been acknowledged by the individual? Does the symptom of heavy-consumption become so dominating, eventually, or interfere to such an extent with the self-conception that it constitutes a main problem; becomes so great and widespread, that the consciousness is over-shadowed by the concrete problem-behaviour which, by that, becomes curtailing for the life-expansion?

From this perspective, the rationale for prevention in general as well as specifically must depart from the joint product of previous experiences and actual life conditions. A presumption, initiating a surpassing of problem-behaviour, must be that the individual will not - unless in case of pathology - place itself in situations purposedly doing harm to him/herself (psychic, somatic, social). A further presumption is the conviction that motion-in-life is present, and that the possibility for change always exists in society and with the individual and potentially is wanted. It is important to include placement in life-cycle and the kind and extension of decisive social network, thus, when one for example estimate in individual connection, if a certain pattern of drinking indicates a risk of developing into an incomprehensible consumption of alcohol.

Hardly, there is any doubt that the development towards a heavy consumption of alcohol has a process-character (Elmeland, Nygaard & Sabroe, 1990), and that prevention therefore is a central activity for a reduction of alcohol related problems. But it is doubtful, if it is possible to phrase it so relatively substantial as Jellinek (1952) when he places a deterministic perspective on the process leading to abuse. As Calahan (1987) points out, longitudinal studies indicate that to know a person have alcohol-related problems at a given time is a poor predictor of the possibility of him/her having alcohol related problems several years ahead.

A research effort to elucidate questions as raised above has to be profound and to have a considerable dimension. A point of departure in the experienced life-situation of the single individual would be a necessity, and these data have to be analysed systematically in the attempt separately and reflected to find significance and meaning of the experiences. The present material does not provide data of such a kind, but some "points of anchoring" and "instantaneous pictures". In the heavy-user analysis to follow, only a few aspects can be elucidated and only at a group and descriptive level.

Basis for data

In article 2 was presented an analysis of the alcohol consumption in relation to the groupings of society. When these data have been presented at conferences, wishes have been expressed from different quarters to have the data analysed from a heavy-drinker perspective. Especially, it has been pointed out that even though the figures presented were correct, it could blur important aspects at a subgroup-level with regard to identifying points of departure for a preventive effort. This aspect was indicated already in the presentation of consumption and social groupings. It was emphasized that the results could only be applied in a group comparison and to indicate, together with other survey data, trends in the development and distribution of the alcohol consumption in the population (ibid.). If considerations of prevention are aimed at blanket - efforts, oriented towards smaller or larger sections of society, average measures of the consumption distributed on comprehensively delimited social variables could be useful in selection of relevant target groups. But it is obvious that the average consumption of the different groupings could be based on dissimilar distributions of the consumption, and a decisive factor could be the relative occurrence on heavy drinkers in the social groups.

Adopting the point of view of heavy drinking does not imply that new sets of data are brought into play, it is the same basic material as presented in article 2, but classified through other principles. In the previous analyses the criteria were the division of society according to certain biological and social factors combined with the calculated average of consumption for the chosen groupings. The heavy-drinker analysis starts from a distinct group of alcohol consumers and describes how this group is compounded with regard to the social groupings of society.

4. Heavy drinkers

Often, it has been discussed if representative surveys of alcohol consumption in reality will cover the heavy drinkers. It is highly probable that with the prevalent data collecting techniques the group "chronic alcohol-dependent" in or out of institutions will only to a slight degree be represented, and if a valid picture should be presented one had to establish special registrations. The other extreme group with regard to alcohol-consumption, the abstainers, one usually find in a representative amount in general surveys. But partly the group of "extreme alcohol consumers" is rather profoundly described in other types of investigations, partly its share of the total consumption of society is little, it is seldom included in general surveys as special group, therefore. When dealing with surveys another problem emerges in relation to heavy drinkers. An underreporting of between 40-60% is common in surveys, and it has been difficult to substantiate, if this underreporting is evenly distributed or, if social, educational or consumer related criteria influence the stated consumption. Presumably, it is not so that deliberate underreporting is a major problem in surveys operating with recalled consumption. In connection with previous data collecting in the project analyses have been carried out to which extent an "average weekly consumption" or even the "consumption of yesterday" was ready concepts for the individual. The results indicated that such measures had to be "calculated" of the interviewee (by retrogressive counting), and that even for shorter periods of time oblivion come about unless you go systematically about it and is supported in your recalling process. The underreporting seems in high degree to be the result of common oblivion and maybe unfamiliar questions related to non-ready concepts (as for example your average weekly consumption).

Moss & Goldstein (1979) point out, that inaccuracies in retrospective data can be related chiefly to errors of memory due to limited memory capacity. There seems to be a higher degree of oblivion as an example, when drinking situations have "low intensity" and are connected to daily life situations with routine character. Inaccuracies also appear, if the reference period for the consumption statements is too short. Frequency and intensity will be important parameters to include in the underreporting discussion, and they are not necessarily in a direct relation to each other. Room (1985) demonstrate as an example that with a low amount of alcohol consumption (< 3 units/week) there is a tendency to overreporting. The low consumption could very well "by definition" mean high intensity in (the few) drinking situations, and Room (ibid.) applies the concept "forward telescoping" to explain the overreporting tendency. It is a problem Sudman and Bradbrun (1982) have taken up, also. They mention that low frequency and high intensity in alcohol consumption seems to result in a "forward telescoping" when the amount for a given reference period is reported. This means that one has tendency to "include" drinking situations in reality placed previous to the reference period. "Backward telescoping" (often related to high level consumption) on the contrary is present in the case you "exclude" consumption from the reference period, resulting in underreporting.

Calculation with regard to the distribution of consumption across the different kinds of beverages indicate a difference in the underreporting. For beer the stated consumption gives an underreporting well over 50%, for wine the figure is 18%. Calculated from representative data these figures could lend substance to the assertion that there is "less awareness" about consumption of the major (and most common) form of alcohol: beer. A relatively greater awareness seems attached to wine consumption, which maybe also is connected with more distinct circumstances as more well-defined periods of time and special occasions. The underreporting for spirits which is just above 50%, maybe could be understood immediately through the fact that with a share of 14% spirits makes up a minor part of the average Dane's alcohol consumption.

In the research project "The Dane's Alcohol Consumer Consciousness" (Sabroe, 1989a, 1991) circumstantial data have been obtained making it possible to calculate a variable named "report-fall". In the project some of the data available from the survey population are of "yesterdays consumption" and for "each day seven days backwards". A figure named "report fall" is calculated as the difference between the mean of the nearest two days' consumption and the two days most distant. Week-ends are excluded due to the special consumption patterns of this period. It is the assumption that a fall of consumption over the two periods can be regarded as a sign of underreporting. If this can be accepted as valid, the analyses indicate a difference with a relatively higher "report-fall" among low-consumers than among high-consumers. This result is not in accordance with Lemmens (1991) who found that there seemed to be a little higher degree of underreporting among high-consumers, but from a different kind of data, however: comparison between diary data and weekly recall data.

Due to the underreporting, it can be difficult to demarcate a heavy-drinker group in the survey population. A high consumption of course can be stipulated from various criteria, and often one would include if the consumption could be assumed to lead to somatic damage and/or to a substantial degree influence the individual's health (in broadest sense), work ability, social relationships and behaviour, etc. A statistical measure as the placing on the distribution related to the populations average ("normal") consumption is seldom seen applied. It is not possible, though, to make individual demarcations from the former mentioned criteria as they are not available data in the project. But in bio-medical connection marginal values have been suggested for a harmful consumption, and - dependent of authority/country - figures ranging from less than one and up to seven-eight units a day have been put forward.

An "unproblematic" (or relatively damage-free) consumption is from some international health authorities placed at ten units per week while other international and national health authorities raise the figure to 15 units a week or even higher (male figure). The Danish Health Council recommend 14 for women and 21 for men as the limit for relatively "risk-free" consumption. For this presentation it has been chosen to delimit the population with a stated consumption of more than twenty units per week. If the underreporting of this group is "traditional" it could mean that the virtual consumption would be of about 40 units/week (or five to six drinks per day). This is a consumption regarded by many experts as potentially damaging. In the present survey this group constitutes six percent. There is no accurate Danish data of the amount of heavy drinkers in the population, but from different sources are suggested estimations in the range of 2.5% to 7%. Compared with such figures, the demarcated group in the survey seems to be "relevant".

5. Heavy drinkers and groups of society

A series of data giving the percentage of heavy drinkers in relation to the customary biographical variables will be brought below. In a following section will be presented cross-analyses using the same variables.

5.1 Heavy-drinker share of subpopulations

5.1.a Sex, age, social group, income

To make the following tables - based on 1988 survey data -more easy to grasp it has been chosen to present the consumption-spectrum in a three-grouping comprising: Less than one unit a week; more than one less than twenty units a week; above twenty units a week. Below the four tables for sex, age, social group are presented. Comments will not be brought with the single tables, but following the tables will be given a presentation of the main results of the analyses.

Table 1: Distribution of consumption groups of men and women (percent)

Sex	Consumption: units per week*		
	<1	> 1 <20 units	>20 units
Men	30.6	51.7	86.7
Women	69.4	48.3	13.3
Ratio (men/women)	1/2.3	1.1/1	6.5/1
p = .0000			

*One unit equals 1.3 cl. 100% alcohol.

Table 2. Age distribution of consumption groups (percent)

Age	Consumption: units per week			Age groups share of population
	< 1	>1 <20	>20	
<20	7.2	6.4	3.8	6.4
21-30	12.8	19.2	14.3	17.6
31-40	17.8	24.4	23.8	23.0
41-50	13.9	19.6	26.7	18.9
51-60	17.5	13.7	19.0	14.8
>61	30.8	16.6	12.4	19.3
	100	100	100	100
p = .000				

Table 3. Social group - distribution in relation to consumption groups (percent)

Social group	Consumption: Units per week			Social group- group's share of population
	< 1	> 1 < 20	> 20	
1	1.1	5.4	11.4	4.9
2	4.7	13.0	13.3	11.3
3	19.2	26.1	32.4	25.0
4	26.4	29.7	23.8	28.7
5	38.6	24.1	19.0	26.8
p = .0000				

Table 4. Income group distribution in relation to consumption groups (percent)

Income group	Consumption: Units per week			Income group's share of population
	< 1	> 1 < 20	> 20	
Low	43.6	24.0	11.4	27.3
Middle	33.9	41.4	26.7	39.0
High	7.2	25.7	50.5	23.4
No answer	15.3	8.9	11.4	10.4
p = .0000				

Based on the tables 1-4 a picture can be drawn, revealing a distinct gender distribution. For the heavy drinker group the ratio *men-women* is 6.5 to 1, while for medium and low range drinkers it is 1.1 to 1 and for the "nothing" group 1 to 2.3. For *social groups* one finds that social group 1 has an *over*representation of heavy drinkers of 58%. Also social group 2 and 3 have an *over*representation of respectively 10% and 23%, while the heavy drinkers are *under*represented in social group 4 and 5 with respectively 18% and 30%. Social group 1 is the upper social group in the stratification scale officially employed by the Danish National Institute of Social Research. Using a tripartition of *income* in a high, medium and low income group it could be demonstrated that the high income group have more than double of heavy drinkers than expected from an even distribution, while the low income group have an underrepresentation of 60%.

5.1.b Occupational groups, branches of trade, political affiliations

The three tables brought below concerning occupational groups, branches of trade and political affiliations will be presented in a form, which partly indicates the recorded amount of heavy drinkers, partly the expected amount regarding the group's share of the population.

For *occupational groups* a picture is obtained showing thrice the amount of heavy drinkers among independents than expected and skilled workers have an *over*representation of 33%. Students, unskilled workers, pensioners and unemployed conversely have an *under*representation of between 25% and 50%.

Table 5. Occupational groups and heavy consumption (percent)

Occupational groups	Occupational groups share of heavy drinkers	Occupational groups share of population
Independent	18.1	6.7
Skilled workers	14.3	9.5
Unemployed	4.8	4.0
Early retired	3.8	3.5
Employees/civil servants	36.2	36.4
Helpmates/married women	1.0	4.2
Unskilled workers	8.6	11.9
Students and pupils	3.8	7.8
Pensioners/out of work	9.5	14.1
Farmers	.0	1.8
	100%	100%

In the spectrum of *political affiliations* (table 6) the Progress Party, Conservatives and Radical Left show an *over*representation of respectively 29%, 23% and 20%, while the Socialist Peoples Party, the Left Party and Social Democrats have an *under*representation of respectively 24%, 20% and 17%.

Table 6. Political affiliations in relation to consumption groups (percent)

Party[1]	The party's share of heavy drinkers	The party's share of population
Progress Party[1]	11.1	15.6
Conservative[2]	18.1	23.3
Radical Left[3]	4.5	5.6
Centrum Democrats[3]	3.2	3.3
Social Democrats[4]	26.5	22.2
Socialist People's Party[5]	13.1	10.0
The Liberal Left[3]	9.7	7.8
Christian People's Party[3]	1.9	.0
Others	11.9	12.2
	100%	100%

1) Positions: 1 = populist, right wing; 2 = right wing; 3 = liberal, right; 4 = centre; 5 = left wing

Finally the distribution according to *branches of trade* gives a picture with two extremes, the Building and Construction sector having more than double the heavy consumers than expected while the Social and Health sector has eight times less.

Table 7: Branches of trades in relation to consumption groups (percent)

Branch	The branch's share of heavy drinkers	The branch's share of population
Building and construction	12.4	5.2
Service	19.0	11.7
Trade	9.5	6.7
Industry	17.1	13.7
Transport (private)	2.9	2.1
Defence and police	1.9	1.3
Public administration	3.8	6.4
Culture	4.8	7.4
Public services (Post, train a.s.o)	1.9	3.1
Agriculture	1.9	3.4
Social/health sector	1.0	8.7
	100%	100%

6. Relational analyses

A series of two sided relational analyses has been carried out, further attempting to uncover characteristics of heavy drinkers. In this connection have been used the above presented variables (sex/age; sex/social group, etc.) related to consumption. No significant relations, according to the criteria of $p < 0.5$, were obtained through these analyses. From the analyses some systematic tendencies in the distributions appeared, however, tendencies which support the previous presented data. In a condensed form these tendencies indicate:

- That heavy drinkers among women as an average are younger (in their thirties) than among men (in their forties and fifties).

- That the amount of heavy drinkers comparatively are highest in the high income group both for men and women.

- That the ratio of heavy drinkers for men-women is most even in the two upper social groups (5 to 1 and 3 to 1). In the two lower the ratio is 10 to 1 and 9 to 1.

- That regardless of age the high income groups has the greatest amount of heavy drinkers.

- That regardless of social group the high income group has the greatest amount of heavy drinkers.

These data - which are *not* statistical proven relations, but only tendencies to systematic relations - are, seen across, concordant and in good relation to the distributions, presented in section 5.

7. Heavy drinking in relation to psycho-social variables

The alcohol questions which are the basis for the present chapter were included in a major survey, in which the themes were: Crisis consciousness, experienced changes in life situation, psychological life quality, resources of acting, changes in life style, attitude to work,, unemployment and the role of state in crisis-combating (Petersen et al., 1989). Preliminarily, it was assumed that connections could be established between a series of these variables and alcohol-consumption. The results proved that only very few statistical significant systematic relations could be found, however. In addition to these were found a few relations in which one could see a tendency to a systematic relation. When alcohol consumption is registered on a fivestep-scale: 0, 1-6, 7-13, 14-20 and above 20 units per week one finds a significant relation between level of consumption and ecological lifestyle: The more oriented towards ecological lifestyle, the higher the consumption. A significant relation is found also between a wish of little control from the state and a high consumption. There is a tendency to a systematic relation between low degree of adaptive resignation and high consumption and between high degree of offensive action and high consumption. When the heavy consumers as a group are compared with the remainder, only one variable obtains significance. For the stress variable the connection is between a high number of stress symptoms and high consumption.

Table 8: Heavy consumption and psychosocial variables

Psychosocial variables	Significant values in relation to heavy consumption
I. Crisis consciousness	
a. Joint responsibility for the crisis	.0813
b. External responsibility for the crisis	.5214
c. Vision of the future	.1682
d. Self-sacrifice	.7264
II. Experienced changes in life situation	.1131
III. Psychological life quality	
a. Personal thriving	.5170
b. Thriving in society	.2098
c. Stress	.0195*
IV. Resources of acting	
a. Offensive action	.8640
b. Adaptive resignation	.0910
V. Changes in style of life	.1114
VI. Attitudes	
a. Attitude to work	.3973
b. Attitude to unemployment	.7874
c. Attitude to the role of the state	.7218

* Systematic relation

8. Discussion

The presented analysis is not a characterization of the heavy-drinker, and if the different variables are placed side by side - with respect to what kind of person is at its summit, one does not acquire any heavy-drinker typology at individual user level. But in a previous analysis (article 2) we took point of departure in the groupings of society and asked how they could be characterized with regard to consumption of alcohol. In the present analysis we have taken another direction, starting from the group defined as heavy drinkers we have asked to which degree we find them in the different groupings of society.

Heavy-drinkers is a concept difficult to demarcate, but it is obvious that, as defined for the analysis it is not the group commonly characterized as "alcoholics" we deal with. It is a group sorted out by a stated consumption, however, that is displayed only by six per cent of the population and a consumption maybe leading to alcohol related problems when considering a customary underreporting assumed to be of a considerable volume.

Designated from these criteria, we find a heavy-drinker group profile that shows a coherent picture then. Heavy-drinkers, as a group, is more than six times as frequent among men than women, but heavy-drinking women are in average younger than men. For men it is the forty and fifty years old, for women it is the thirty years old. It is in the higher social groups one find relatively most heavy-drinkers, and the ratio men-women for these groups approach the "normal" consumption ratio of three to one, whereas the heavy-drinker ratio of men-women in the lower social groups is nine to one. Crosswise of sex and social groups it is the high income group, which relatively seen have most heavy consumers, and these also are more frequent in higher placed occupational groups. For branches of trade the Construction and Building sector has twice as many heavy drinkers as expected, while the Social and Health sector shows eight times less than expected.

Comparison between this heavy-drinker picture and the picture obtained from the distribution of the general consumption in the groups of society reveals obvious similarities. From the analysis of the general consumption it was concluded that in the Danish society a high level consumption could not be seen as an expression of a "poverty-culture" (a prevalent prejudice), rather it could be regarded as an "affluence-phenomenon". It was the wealthy, the higher social groups, the higher occupations which accounted for the relatively highest consumption by groups. An average consumption like this of course can be compounded in different ways, and it could be of importance to establish the place of heavy drinkers in this picture, not the least from a prevention-perspective. And when the heavy drinkers are brought into focus, we find that they relatively more frequent are found in the social groups which also display a relatively high general consumption. Relatively seen, heavy drinkers are found to a higher degree in the groups comfortably off than in the less well-paid groups of society.

Additional to the analysis applying the socio-biographical variables relations between consumption and the psychosocial variables from the "Crisis-project" were analysed (Petersen et al., 1989). Only very few significant relations appeared, one being a systematic relation between ecological style of life and alcohol consumption, indicating a relation between high level of consumption and low degree of ecological life style. Moreover there was a tendency to a relation between a low level of alcohol-consumption and adaptive resignation and between high level of alcohol consumption and outward action. Three-sided analyses between these variables, consumption and "sociological" variables as for example social-group indicate, that the latter dominates compared with the "psychological" variables. As the "psychological" variables are defined and operationalized in the crisis-project, they seem to be related to alcohol-consumption only to a minor extent. It is obviously the social important aspects of the individual's characteristics and the socially decisive life circumstances, which are significant in relation to an alcohol-consumption, also from a heavy-drinker perspective. The individual is the creator of his/her own social interplays, but at the same time these interplays are framed for the individual. Taken apart both conditions are true, not in isolation, but as parts of a dynamic unity.

Overall, the results seems to indicate a relationship expressing that given groupings of society with different average per capita consumption, the relative amount of heavy-consumers will follow the level of this average consumption. The results seems, in this sense then, indirectly to support the general idea of the hypothesis formulated by Ledermann (1956) that a relationship can be established between the incident of alcohol related problems and the per capita consumption in a given population. At least if heavy-consumption per se is regarded as a problem even having not provoked treatment-seeking behaviour.

It is important to remember, that the picture presented above is drawn from a comparison of the relative conditions of social groupings. If taking the social group criteria, social group 3 will constitute five times as many as social group 1 in the representative population. Regardless of the lower ratio (see table three), social group 3 will count nominally for three times as many heavy-consumers as social group 1, nevertheless.

In a prevention perspective the many facets, constituting the heavy-consumer picture, must be implicated, including the way they can be identified with regard to familiar social groupings. As discussed in section 1 and 2, an overall (comprehensive) approach in the preventive work is essential, an approach which at the societal level have to consider among other things the significance of the social environment and socio-demographic characteristics, with which the target group of the prevention efforts can be identified.

References

Cahalan, D. (1987). *Understanding America's drinking problem*. San Fransisco: Jossey-Bass.

Edwards, G. (1982). *The treatment of drinking problems*. London: Grant, McIntyre.

Edwards, G. et al. (1977). *Alcohol related disabilities*. Geneva: World Health Organization.

Elmeland, K., Nygaard, P., Sabroe, K.-E. (1990). Storbrugere. 12 fortællinger om alkoholbrug. *Psykologisk Skriftserie Aarhus, vol. 15, no. 1.* (Heavy drinkers. 12 stories on alcohol consumption.)

Jellinek, E. (1952). Phases of alcohol addiction. *Quart.Journ.Studies Alcohol, 13*, 673-684.

Ledermann, S. (1956). *Alcool, Alcoolisme, Alcoolisation*. Données scientifique de charactère physiologue, économique et social. Paris: Presse Universitaires de France.

Lemmens, P. (1991). *Measurements and distributions of alcohol consumption*. Den Haag: CIP-Gegevens Koninklijke Bibliotheek.

Moss, L. & Goldstein, H. (eds.) 1979). *The recall methods in social sciences*. London: Institute of Education.

Petersen, E., Andersen, J.G., Larsen, J.D., Sabroe, K.-E. & Sommerlund, B. (1989). *De krisebevidste og offervillige danskere*. Aarhus: Psykologisk Institut. (The crisis-conscious and self-sacrificing Danes.)

Plant, M. (1979). *Drinking Careers*. London: Tavistock.

Room, R. (1985). Measuring alcohol consumption in the US. Paper ICAA/ ALCOHOL EPIDEMIOLOGY MEETING. Rome.

Sabroe, K.-E. (1989a). Alcohol Consumer Consciousness. A social psychological approach to alcohol. Oslo: National Directorate for Prevention of Alcohol and Drug Problems. 35th ICAA, vol. IV, 1-21.

Sabroe, K.-E. (1989b). Alkohol og samfundets grupperinger. In E. Petersen, J.G. Andersen, J.D. Larsen, K.-E. Sabroe & B. Sommerlund (1989). *De krisebevidste og offervillige danskere*. Aarhus: Psykologisk Institut. (Alcohol and the groupings of society.)

Sabroe, K.-E. (1991). Alkohol, lav pris, tilgængelighed - øget forbrug? *Nordisk Alkohol Tidsskrift, 1, no. 2.* (Alcohol, low price, availability - increased consumption?

Sudman, S. & Bradburn, N. (1982). Asking questions. San Fransisco: Jossey-Bass.

Vaillant, G.E. (1983). *The national history of alcoholism*. Cambridge, M.A.: Harvard University Press.

WHO (1952). *Technical Report Series, no. 48* (Mental Health: 2nd Report of Alcoholism Subcommittee.

5.

ALCOHOL AND WORK

ALCOHOL AND WORK

I. Introduction

The human activity: *work* plays an essential role for the frame of understanding of the project "The Danes' Alcohol Consumer Consciousness". In a double sense work is an element in what could be characterized as the individual's identity, both as the society - created frame for it, but also as the concrete life-activity, which is an expression of the individual's choice within that frame. Even in to-day's leisure-oriented society the work has maintained its place as identity creating factor.

The Alcohol Consumer Consciousness has its basis in an understanding of consciousness as being a product of man's relationship with the social and physical environment. It is through the consciousness the individual cognitively and emotionally relates to his surroundings. The relations with the surroundings have the character of a life-activity, which is necessary for the individual's life-upholding and the work constitutes a substantial life activity in our society.

In a historical perspective alcohol and work have always been coupled with social attitudes, covering a broad area of opinions from appropriate/necessary to inappropriate/unnecessary. The two sets of characteristics could almost be the starting and (provisional) ending point of a line covering the last couple of hundred years. In today's Denmark alcohol and work have again been a major issue after a quiet period. If the debate shall reach beyond the myths, information, as in this article, will be an imperative necessity.

In a survey, which comprises a greater population, one must always compromise, not the least of economical reasons. Complex variables of investigation - as for example the concept of consciousness - also cause that optimal data collection seldom (never) is obtainable. It became the case also with regard to the alcohol and work data in this project. As mentioned work was considered essential in operationalizing the alcohol consumer consciousness concept, but there also was the limitation that the amount of questions available could not exceed six. We decided that consumption in the workplace had to be included and furthermore that two subjects should be elucidated: Alcohol policy in regard to work and the extent of and intervention in alcohol related problems at the work place.

2. Data material

In a major survey on alcohol collected in April 1989, including 2,000 Danes, six questions concerned consumption in the work situation, knowledge of colleagues with a great alcohol consumption, experience of how the reactions were towards a great alcohol consumption in the work situation and whether the workplace ought to have an alcohol policy.

In the following presentation a preliminary analysis will be given of the frequency-distributions of the questions, supplemented with some initial cross-analyses with background variables. Further analyses will be brought in a later publication bringing a total presentation of the results.

The population studied is - due to the special circumstances into which it enters - compounded in such a way that it consists of a representative national sample of 1000 and a representative sample of 1000 drawn from Vejle County. The reason for this division is that Vejle County is the Danish community that enters into the WHO-Europe initiative of "Community response to alcohol related problems". This again is part of the WHO activities established in relation to the "Health for all year 2000" objectives. Besides Denmark 14 other European countries participate in the WHO-initiative.

A comparison of the two populations of 1000 on essential variables as sex, age and occupation indicates that they are statistically identical. For a few other variables there are minor differences. A comparison on selected dependent variables also indicates that the two populations are comparable, even though minor, unsystematic differences are found. In this preliminary analysis, it has been chosen to combine the two populations in order to get a data foundation of 2000 and to accept the lesser uncertainty in the table-material this will cause in relation to a general representativity, rather than to use the two statistically inferior samples of 1000.

The investigation has been carried out as a telephone-interviewing (with the assistance of the data collection agency AIM), and the questions gave partly the possibility of a quantitative registration of the answers and partly a greater amount of questions were open, leading up to a qualitative analysis. The questions related to work are four of the first category, while one is open and one gives the possibility of supplementary answers.

The results presented below are all highly significant, and this is of course an essential ascertainment as the formulation of statements rests upon it. But the matter of significance would not be persued further for statistical purposes.

2.1. Alcohol consumption in the workplace

The question on the frequency of alcohol consumption in the workplace was worded: "How often do you drink alcohol in your workplace?" The respondent was free to choose the time-period he/she wished to use, the interviewer being prepared to offer the below indicated categories.

In table 1 is shown the distribution for the total population. It is a small number of workplaces in which a prohibition of alcohol has been introduced. But, almost 50% of the respondents declare on the other side that they *never* drink alcohol at work and an additional 31.5% state a minor amount comparing to at *the most a couple of times* a month. It is not asked how much is drunk in the workplace, but if we compare with the data which can be derived from the questions of the distribution of the consumption throughout the 24 hours of the day, the amount drunk supposedly must be insignificant. A further analysis will be carried out in connection with a later reporting (cf. Sabroe, 1993).

Table 1: Alcohol consumption in the workplace

Frequency	Total %	Sex	
		Women %	Men %
1 Daily	3.9	0.3	7.5
2 A couple of times/week	5.4	1.3	9.5
3 One time/week	7.1	4.0	10.2
4 A couple of times/month	6.2	3.9	8.5
5 One time/month	5.1	5.1	5.0
6 A couple of times/year	4.7	5.9	3.6
7 One time/year	1.6	1.8	1.4
8 Only special occasions	13.9	15.8	12.1
9 Never	49.2	59.3	39.5
10 Alcohol prohibition	2.0	1.5	2.4
11 Don't know	.8	1.0	.5
12 Refuse to answer	0.1	0.1	0
	100	51.3	48.7

A little less than 4% of the respondents daily drink alcohol at work. This group could together with those who drink a couple of times a week (5.4%) maybe constitute a potential problem group in the workplace.

It is important to be aware of the fact that the question was formulated in general (in the workplace). It is not possible to conclude, therefore, that the consumption takes place during the work itself, it could just as well be in connection with lunch or other types of meal break. But even a consumption during breaks could be problematic obviously with regard to given work-tasks.

As said above no stated figures from the respondents are available for the amount consumed in the workplace, but a question, about knowledge of colleagues with a high consumption of alcohol and intervention (at work) confronted with the problem, could indicate that a group exists with alcohol problems in the workplace (see p. 97). Even so it is unsupported to claim from these figures that the group of employees (and independents) with a work alcohol problem should be as big as the approx. 10%, which comprises the weekly or more frequent drinkers. Enjoying alcohol in the amount of 1-2 times a week at work in connection with a break (in so far as it is a small amount) could hardly be called potentially critical from a workplace misuse perspective, possibly being inappropriate/critical in a given work relation though.

The presented results are in agreement in general with the results from Colling (1989) in the sense that they de-dramatize the assertion that workplaces are high-consumption areas. But it seems that the present investigation - which represents the single employee's (and employer's) own statements/experiences - indicates a slightly more favourable picture than the results obtained by Colling from 4000 representatively chosen work places, in which the mail-distributed question-naires to a high degree were completed by the management and dealt with the workplace in general. The problem of differences in statements on own behaviour versus general behaviour is shortly commented p. 117. From the current debate - as it is represented in the media - a common impression is, however, that when the myths have been put aside there is not much to support the view that the workplace is a problem area with regard to alcohol consumption. It clearly appears that the leisure-sphere is the potential heavy consumption domain. A new recognition on the other hand seems to be that the place of work could be important with regard to a rational prevention in relation to a high consumption in the leisure time. Alcohol consumption habits or traditions in the leisure time could originate in the workplace. At the same time the workplace is an important identity creating factor, and thereby central in a rational prevention.

2.1.1. Sex

As in the general pattern of consumption one also in the work situation finds *significant* differences between men and women. From table 1 it appears that the difference is especially pronounced when the more frequent consumption is the case. Among those who state that they daily drink alcohol at work *96% are men* and only *4% women*, and out of the respondents who drink a couple of drinks a week, 88% are men and 12% women. When the question is abstinence or the more scarce consumption at work the differences are far less, still displaying the same tendency, however, being greater abstinence for women. Although the figures are small, it is worth while noting that women do not report greater restrictivity (alcohol prohibition) in their workplaces than do men; the differences uncovered seem to indicate different styles of life.

2.1.2. Age

The results from this investigation is a "snapshot", and it is impossible therefore to say anything about an age determined development regarding the alcohol consumption. To acquire important information like that, longitudinal research or "trend-analysis" is indispensable. The picture shown in table 2 gives evidence of a profile nevertheless, which is recognizable from recent Danish research on the common alcohol consumption - even though the pictures are not identical. There is reason to make a point of the results therefore, as being a manifestation of how the alcohol consumption appears in Danish workplaces, perceived from an age angle.

It is the *20* and the *30 years* old followed by the *40 years* old, who have the relatively most frequent consumption of alcohol at work. Just short of 1/5 of the 20 and 30 years old and 1/6 of the 40 years old consume alcohol at least one time a week at work, while the figure for the 50 and 60 years age groups are about 1/8. Conversely it is more than 4 out of 5 of the young below the age of 20, who *never* or *extremely seldom* consume alcohol at work, and from 108 respondents below 20 only one stated to do it daily.

Table 2: Alcohol in the workplace according to age (percentage)

	alcohol-prohib.	daily	cpl. times/ week	one time /week	cpl. times/ month	one time /month	cpl. times/ year	one time /year	only special occ.	never	do not know	will not answer	Total
15-19	4.2	1.0	2.1	6.3			3.1		10.4	72.9			6.1
20-29	1.7	2.3	6.6	11.7	6.3	7.1	6.3	1.4	10.3	46.2	0.3		22.2
30-39	2.5	4.2	7.2	8.0	9.0	5.5	4.2	1.7	14.0	42.6	.7	.2	25.4
40-49	1.7	5.0	5.2	5.2	6.9	6.9	5.2	2.5	17.1	43.1	1.1		22.9
50-59	2.2	6.0	3.0	4.3	5.2	3.4	3.0	0.9	16.4	54.7	0.9		14.7
60-69		3.5	5.3	3.5	1.8		6.2	1.8	13.3	63.7	0.9		7.2
70-89				4.0	4.0				12.0	76.0	4.0		1.6
Total	2.0	3.9	5.4	7.2	6.2	5.1	4.7	1.6	13.9	49.2	0.8	0.1	100.0

The percentage of respondents, which - relatively seen - state at least one time a week consumption of alcohol at work drop from the group over 20 years with rising age. In the distribution of the *general* consumption (presented in article 2) the age group of the forties has a significantly higher consumption than the other age groups. This picture is supported by the general consumption figures from the survey from which the results in this report also are taken. It seems thus that a different consumption pattern exists for the age groups depending on whether the consumption is related to work or to leisure time, with more young having a relatively frequent consumption at work.

2.1.3. Occupation

A previous investigation (article 2) revealed a significant difference between occupations (and also branches of trade) with regard to consumption of alcohol in general. In table 3 the distribution of alcohol consumption in the workplace according to occupation is shown. It indicates significant differences, which again reflect the tendency from the common consumption.

Table 3: Alcohol in the workplace according to occupation (percentage)

	alcohol-prohib.	daily	cpl. times/ week	one time /week	cpl. times/ month	one time /month	cpl. times/ year	one time /year	only special occ.	never	do not know	will not answer	Total
Skilled worker	1.4	10.1	8.0	11.2	8.0	5.4	4.3	2.2	10.9	38.4			17.4
Independent	2.0	6.1	5.1	3.1	4.1	2.0	4.1	2.0	13.3	56.1	2.0		6.2
Unskilled worker	3.1	3.5	3.9	3.9	5.0	4.2	6.9	1.2	12.4	55.2	0.8		16.4
Farmer (indep.)		2.7	8.1	8.1		2.7	2.7		8.1	64.9	2.7		2.3
Employee /civil serv.	1.5	2.6	6.8	6.6	8.2	6.8	5.1	1.4	18.2	42.4	0.3		41.0
Appren./stud. /pupil.	3.6	.5	.5	10.7	3.1	3.6	3.6	2.0	10.7	60.7	.5	.5	12.4
Helpmate			3.8	7.7				3.8	3.8	73.1	7.7		1.6
Housewife									6.5	90.3	3.2		2.0
Refuse to answer										90.9	9.1		.7
Total	2.0	3.9	5.4	7.1	6.2	5.1	4.7	1.6	13.9	49.2	.8	.1	100.0

There are significantly *fewer* from the skilled workers and from employees/civil servants who *"never* drinks at work" than from the remainder occupations. If the employees/civil servants are divided into a higher and lower placed group of the administrative hierarchy, a tendency to more with a higher consumption among the highest placed appears, the picture of alcohol consumption as an affluence-phenomenon is thus maintained in the workplace data.

If one, reversely, looks at the daily consumption it is the *skilled workers* who top the ranking with the *independent* following. At all, the skilled workers are high in all consumption frequencies down to one time a month. Also employees/civil servants are in a high position on these consumption frequencies, whereas this is not the case for the independent contrary to expectations. When compared with other results (article 2) on the consumption of this group, it must be considered if the workplace has been interpreted as the concrete physical place at which work is done and not including business lunch or activities alike outside the workplace.

If we go beyond the "frequent" (daily) consumption and look at the consumption of 1-2 times alcohol consumption per week, we get a distribution a little unusual compared with the traditional picture. True enough, skilled workers are at the top, but the following groups traditionally are placed as low consumption groups - and also are in the overall consumption figures of this investigation - it is the farmers, the apprentices/students and helpmates. It must be remembered, however, that these figures cover only 8-20% of the respective populations, and do *not* warrant a *group characteristic*. As with the previous data the value lies in the possibility of comparison *between* groups.

3. Access to alcohol in the workplace

A central theme in the Nordic debate on prevention of alcohol related problems is the question of alcohol free zones in society, taken up by among others the Nordic Council (Nordisk Råd, 1988). And in the Danish debate the question of the place of work as an alcohol free zone has the ear of the media, and brings some parties of the labour market to the barricades. The arguments have varied from common health reasons, over safety- and risk reasons to reasons of productivity. It is not always clear where the front-line runs, if it is the traditional division in employers/employees, or if it is the labour market confronted an external influence or if the problem is a question of enroachment on degrees of freedom rather than a wish of having the possibility of obtaining alcohol at work. In the recent years the debate seems, however, to have been brought out of the traditional controversy sphere between employers and workers, and taken up in a wellfare/health (and productivity) connection (Sabroe, 1993).

A question presented to the respondents gave the possibility of answering if there ought to be free, limited or no access to alcohol in the workplaces in Denmark. Table 4 presents the distribution of answers according to occupation.

Table 4: Access to alcohol in the workplace according to occupation (percentage)

	Free access	Limited access	No access	Don't know	Will not answer	Total
Skilled worker	14.6	42.5	36.4	6.4		14.0
Employee/civil serv.	10.2	52.5	32.0	4.5	0.8	32.5
Independent	9.1	42.4	42.4	5.1	1.0	4.9
Unskilled worker	8.0	43.1	45.0	3.8		13.0
Unempl./pensioners/early retired	5.8	37.4	49.2	7.6		19.0
Appren./stud./pupil	5.4	55.1	34.6	4.9		10.2
Farmer	5.3	39.5	50.0	5.3		1.9
Housewife	4.4	17.8	75.6	2.2		2.2
Helpmate		37.9	62.1			1.4
Refuse to answer	16.7	41.7	41.7			.6
Total	8.8	45.5	40.2	5.2	.3	100.0

The distinctive result is, that only *a very little minority* (8.8%) wishes *free access* to alcohol at work. It is furthermore worth to remark that in broad outline the rank order is as for the consumption distribution. A little more than 45% of the respondents are of the opinion that there should be a limited access to alcohol at the places of work. These two groups combined give *a slight majority to those who want to have alcohol available* in the workplace.

It is among the unskilled workers, farmers, the unemployed, pensioners, early retired and housewives that one finds the greatest support of *prohibition against alcohol* at work. For the unskilled workers it is close to be an equal number, who wants and does not want to have access to alcohol, for the remainder there is a majority for prohibition. The highest *support for alcohol* in the workplace comes from employees/civil servants followed by apprentices/students (who by the way is a low consumption group), skilled workers and independents. Cf. also the results from Sabroe (1991) which support the above given figures and analyses.

4. Alcohol problems and work

It often is seen that to acknowledge having alcohol problems is late acquired, but also that becoming aware of problems of other people is more easy, even though it does not necessarily lead to actions regarding help/support or the like to the person having problems. The latter applies to both fellow employees and management.

In the investigation was asked, if the respondent at the present or previous workplaces had known a person with a high consumption of alcohol. "High consumption" was chosen instead of "abuse" in order not to create associations to extreme situations alone, one would expect the reporting to be rather high therefore. An inevitable result of high figures also stem from the condition that the information concerns both present and previous workplaces, and that the time-perspective is a person's entire work-life must result in high figures inevitably.

Table 5 shows that just over 50% state that they have had contact in a workplace with a person having a high consumption of alcohol.

Table 5: Work colleagues with a high alcohol consumption according to occupation (percentage)

	Yes	No	Don't know	Refuse to answer	Total
Skilled worker	62.5	36.8	.4	.4	14.0
Employee/civil serv.	61.0	38.4	0.6		32.5
Unskilled worker	53.8	45.0	1.2		13.0
Independent	50.5	46.5	3.0		4.9
Unemployed	39.7	54.7	5.3	.3	19.0
Appren./stud./pupil	38.5	54.6	6.8		10.2
Helpmate	34.5	58.6	6.9		1.4
Farmer	13.2	78.9	7.9		1.9
Housewife	11.1	71.1	15.6	2.2	2.2
Refuse to answer	25.0	75.0			.6
Total	50.8	46.2	2.8	.1	100.0

It is the relatively high consumating groups again, who most frequently state that they have had work colleagues with a high alcohol consumption. Furthermore, it was asked if there were any interventions in regard to the person with alcohol problems. For the groups which reported the greatest frequency of high consumers, it seems to have happened in about 50% of the cases, with employees/civil servants as the most frequent (58%). When an intervention took place, it mainly came from *management* (about two thirds of the cases) and the supplementary answers clearly show a dominance of *caution* or *sacking*. In almost one third of the cases the respondent *himself or colleagues* intervened, but only rather seldom (5% of the cases) intervention had come from *shop stewards*. The figures are small (intervenitons are mentioned of about 500), and therefore should be assessed with caution. But there appears not to be any greater difference between the above mentioned groups of occupation in relation to the indicated general pattern. The figures in relation to sanctions and who reacts when a high consumption is ascertained, are in accordance with Colling (1989).

5. Summing up

The results from a representative survey of 2000 Danes seem *not* to indicate that alcohol is the major problem in Danish workplaces in the way it often has been voiced in the media within the last years. There is a high degree of consistency in the information, acquired from the different parts of the investigation. With regard to the amount of consumption accordance also exists in relation to other greater surveys (cf. article 1). *Only just under four out of every hundred daily consume alcohol at work*, but the *men* - as it is a fact for the common consumption - carry the main responsibility for the consumption with more than *seven out of every hundred*. It is the twenty to fifty ear old men in particular, who drink alcohol at work, and with regard to occupation the skilled workers and independents top the list with respectively ten and six out of every hundred, who daily consume alcohol at work.

The question if alcohol at all ought to be in the workplaces divides the population in such a way that *a little majority is in favour of access to alcohol.* But *less than nine out of every hundred are of the opinion that access should be free*, while just over two fifths of the population find that access should be limited, and two out of five adopt the idea of prohibition. It is the skilled workers and employees/civil servants, who to the highest degree support free or limited access.

Half the population has - during her/his work life - worked with a colleague, who had a high alcohol consumption. It is a big figure - which could seem to be in contradiction to the above mentioned figures - but supposedly the figure reflects the wording of the question, and that it is a question of lifetime information. Interventions have been undertaken in about half of the reported cases, primarily from management and also to some extent from work colleagues, but relatively seldom from shop stewards.

6. Discussion

In a Danish connection the question of alcohol and work has in the recent years been dealt with in Sælan (1984); Hansen & Andersen (1985), Århus Amtskommune (1988), Colling (1989), and Sabroe (1993). Furthermore Nielsen (1982) has referred to the subject indirectly, indicating that 23% of the Danes on a given work day have had alcohol in their lunch hour. The subject has been most extensively elucidated in an investigation from The National Social Research Institute (SFI), which comprised 4000 Danish workplaces (Colling, 1989). With regard to the overall picture, drawn of the relation alcohol-work, there is a great overlap with the results in the present investigation: alcohol seems not to be a problem at the great majority of Danish workplaces. Some aspects seem a little more problematically presented in the SFI-investigation, in which the mail-distributed questionnaires in more than 4 out of 5 workplaces were answered by the management, but the differences are not significant. The previous investigations (Sælan, 1984; Hansen & Andersen, 1985) indicate a somewhat higher consumption at the workplaces, than do the present investigation, Århus Amtskommune (1988) and Colling (1989). Sælan (1984) states, thus, that about one third of the total consumption presumedly is related to the work situation and Hansen & Andersen (1985) record, that 15% of the men and 2% of the women on a random work day have had alcohol at work. The respective results have been obtained with different methodology and populations and therefore are difficult to compare. But it seems, however, that there is support for a continuation of the tendency, suggested by Hansen & Andersen (1985), that a change takes place altering the consumption pattern of a previous frequent day-consumption in the work place to a predominant pattern of consumption during the evenings and especially during the weekends. This assumption will be substantially supported by data in a forthcoming publication from the project (Sabroe & Rasmussen, 1994, in print).

The above given representative results have a certain interest, not the least because the last few years have witnessed a debate in the media, which more has been founded on myths and suppositions than real information. The debate has singled out alcohol as a considerable problem for the labour market, and claimed that solutions were difficult because of the attitudes (especially among employees) regarding a regulation (often expressed as prohibition) of access to alcohol in the workplace. From the investigation a picture can be drawn now, indicating that the debate has been somewhat distorted, at least with regard to the amount of consumption. Assertions to the effect that one third of the total Danish alcohol consumption is related to the workplace (Alkohol Debat, 1985) thus seem to be far off. It will be essential henceforth to remember, that irrespective of the fact that only a very few workplaces have alcohol prohibition, it is a little minority for whom alcohol at work *could* seem to be a problem (the daily users which amounts to scarcely 4%) . The hypothetical form and the word problem (instead of abuse) is used by purpose, because nothing in the above given results indicates the extent of the daily consumption. An estimation will be obtained in a coming analysis, in which the common consumption (distributed across the 24 hours of the day) and the consumption frequency at work will be combined.

But irrespective of the dimension of the problem, a pattern clearly emerges of a workplace consumption which reflects the common consumption. The universal socio-economic relationships rather than the characteristics of the workplace seem to determine the consumption, although it is possible to draw a consistent picture in relation to the consumption of the different groups of occupation. The pattern of consumption indicates that a preventive effort should be aimed at the leisure sector, but that the workplace could be an important media for such an effort.

A local investigation has been undertaken at several work places in Aarhus County (Aarhus Amtskommune, 1988). Representativity was not met in this investigation, and the amount of participants were rather low. But the main results are nevertheless in agreement with the results from the present investigation. Results from the Aarhus investigation have initiated a debate in the county with the participation of the health authorities and the parties of the labour market, a debate aiming at a co-operative attitude, but the positions have been traditionally marked and often related to the question of prohibition. A practical result of the county investigation has been production of a prevention-kit, containing information and debate material - which is freely distributed to workplaces in the county. A similar kit has been produced by the International Labourers Organization (ILO) in co-operation with WHO (ILO, 1986).

If the question of an eventual regulation of alcohol in the workplaces is maintained there are results, which could contribute to an elucidation of the media-debate. Notwithstanding, that there is a scanty consumption, a little majority nevertheless wants to maintain the possibility of having this consumption. *But far the main part (more than 9 out of every 10) is prepared for a regulation of alcohol in the workplace* and important it also is to remember, that *just over 40% of the Danish labour force want to have prohibition of alcohol in the workplace.*

7. Postscript

In Sabroe (1993), the Danish part of an international investigation of "Alcohol and drugs in the workplace" is reported. In this investigation, representatives from ten employers' and workers' organizations and seven major enterprises were interviewed parallel to answering a greater questionnaire. The report supports the picture presented in this article and further presents information on the area of alcohol policies in the enterprises. Since 1989 initiatives both from the Danish Confederation of Worker's Unions and Danish Employer's Confederation and from a greater part of especially enterprises with more than fifty employees have resulted in establishment of alcohol policies in the workplaces regulating or prohibiting alcohol consumption.

References

Colling, H. (1989) *Alkohol og arbejdsliv.* København: Socialforskningsinstituttet. (Alcohol and work life)

Hansen, E.J. & Andersen, D. (1985) *Alkoholforbrug og Alkoholpolitik.* København: Socialforskningsinstituttet. (Alcohol consumption and alcohol policy.)

ILO (1986) Responses to *Drug and Alcohol problems in the work place.* Geneve: International Labour Office.

Nordisk Råd (1988): *Medlemsforslag A 846/S.* (Member suggestions, Nordic Council)

Sabroe, K.-E. (1989) Alkohol og samfundets grupperinger (kap. 4) I Petersen, E., Andersen, J., Dalberg-Larsen, J., Sabroe, K.-E. & Sommerlund, B. *De krisebevidste og offervillige danskere.*Århus: Psykologisk Institut. (Alcohol and groupings of society)

Sabroe, K.-E. (1988) *Alcohol Consumer Consciousness. A social psychological perspective.* Oslo: National Directorate for the Prevention of Alcohol and Drug problems. Proceedings 35th ICAA, vol. IV. 1-21.

Sabroe, K.E. (1991). Alkoholforbrugets udviklng 1988-90. In E. Petersen et al. *De trivsomme og arbejdsomme danskere.* Århus: Aarhus Universitetsforlag (The Thriving and Work-eager Danes).

Sabroe, K.-E. (1993) Alcohol and drugs in the workplace. Danish data. Report to ILO, Geneva in connection with an ILO/EC DG5 project (in print).

Sabroe, K.-E. & Rasmussen, O. (1994). *Danskernes alkoholforbrugerbevidsthed* (in print).

Sælan, H. Alkohol og Arbejdsliv. *Alkoholdebat* (1985) April, *no. 20.* København: Alkohol- og Narkotikarådet. (Alcohol and life of work)

Århus Amtskommune (1988) *Forsøgsprojekt alkohol og arbejdsmiljø.* Århus: Århus Amtskommune, mimeo, 63 s. (Pilot project: Alcohol and working conditions)

6.

REASONS FOR DRINKING /NOT DRINKING ALCOHOL

REASONS FOR DRINKING/NOT DRINKING ALCOHOL

> *To live inattentively is immoral. Moral is to live attentively, this means listening to other people but also to oneself.*
>
> (Krzysztof Kieslowski, Polish film instructor)

1. Introduction

In the running research project: "Danes during the Crisis" (Petersen et al, 1987, 1989), in which the author is participating, the 1988 survey made it possible to include a few questions about alcohol. There were three sets of questions: One question of weekly mean consumption, three questions of associations to the concepts beer, wine and spirits, and two questions of "reasons to drink" respectively "reasons not to drink" alcohol. It is the latter two questions which will be dealt with in this article. The data are based on a representative population of 1,810 persons between 16-75 years (Petersen et al., 1989, annex 4).

2. Causes to drink

When the question "why do people drink" is asked, the immediate reaction will be: "That many reasons can be given" irrespective of whether the question is asked in a lay or scientific connection. It is so also that if one compares the reasons given within either a lay or a scientific context, dominating patterns will prevail. But there is a merging between lay and scientific understanding, this without regard to the fact that the lay understanding is a manifestation of immediate and implicit "theories", while the scientific understanding builds on mediate processing and explicit theoretical models.

This merging and this discrepancy by way of introduction are emphasized because the ultimate goal for the project "The Danes' Alcohol Consumer Consciousness" - of which the results to be presented are a part - is to promote an understanding of how alcohol as subject is in evidence of Danes in general, and how they relate to this subject (Sabroe, 1989). Besides contributing to the general extension of understanding, the knowledge is intended to be used in a preventive connection. With regard to this, knowledge is important which conceptions are predominant of why people drink or not drink alcohol. A rational prevention must always start from that concrete knowledge of, from those beliefs about and from the emotional involvement in the subject, which are identifiable in the population dealt with.

It is a problem - at least in a Danish connection - when you raise a question with the wording "why people drink (alcohol)". In the Danish language there are connotations of the word "drink", which maybe is subcultural in relation to their penetration, but in which there is, nevertheless, an underlying tendency across the subcultural stratification. A connotation of this kind is, that the word "drink" has a negative loading, when used in connection with alcohol, understood the way that if "one drinks" (alcohol) one is in a heavy-user category. If the question "reasons for drinking alcohol" is used in a survey relation, it must be considered that some answers could be influenced by this negative connotation. It is evident, although, that the semantic content would presumably be differently apprehended in the two phrases "he drinks" and "he drinks alcohol", with more negative connotations to the former. It is also worthwhile mentioning that in daily Danish language alcohol, literally translated, is characterized as "means of enjoyment" and "to drink alcohol" could without problems be expressed as "to enjoy" alcohol. This is the case in e.g. German also, but not in Anglo-Saxon connection and of course is a cultural fact to be considered.

It is an interesting problem which relationship exists between the formal scientific and the lay understanding of "why people drink alcohol", of which I have not been able to find documentation in the literature, although there has been a certain interest for lay theories on alcoholism and their relation to formal theories (Furnham & Lowick, 1984). But it is obvious from folklore and literary descriptions that, as an example through this century, there has been a shift from moral-oriented to illness or social-origin viewpoints among common man also. "Also" naturally refers to the fact that one can see a parallel development in the scientific world, "forestalling" the general sociocultural movements. This relationship could be interesting regarding preventive endeavours. That is, if there exists a "cultural gap or cultural delay" of greater extent between the understanding of those, who is in command of the preventive enterprises, and the understanding which is predominant in the population in general or among subcultural target groups. A related problem is the relationship between the penal legislation and the public sentiment of justice or more general between legislation (for example about alcohol) and the prevalent opinions in the population (of price, availability, control etc.), in which case experienced/registered differences could be one of more reasons to appoint legislation-amendment commissions. Olsson (1990) has dealt with this problem in a discussion of the legitimacy of alcohol policy.

As I have indicated, it is an important topic of research to try to illuminate what is the origin of prevailing opinions of "why people drink alcohol". It is important because acquisition of beliefs regarding causes and processes can be of central significance not only with regard to the "general to commit oneself" but also for the political making up of mind, and for the professional prevention and treatment efforts. Formal theories and the general political attitudes, and the praxis derived herefrom, will be governing for these endeavours, but, as a fact, the common opinions exist and they will be present in the situations in which the formal points of view are applied.

It is not an easy task to establish an analysis of this relationship, the picture drawn by the "cultural trend setting", formal theories of the alcohol area, is exceedingly variegated. If we again take the extreme consumption situation, which is commonly named alcoholism, we find conflicting views, which will bring confusion presented to common man. The three major areas of understanding: biology, psychology, and sociology have been basis for as well single discipline as cross-disciplinary oriented views of causality with regard to excessive use of alcohol (Room, 1974: Edwards & Grant, 1978; Buus-Jensen, 1981; Mansell Pattison & Kaufman, 1982; Mandell, 1983; Flensted-Nielsen & Evers, 1984). There are views, in single-discipline connections, which "state" that 1) alcoholics are biological predestined to develop an alcohol dependence, 2) that acquired psychological dispositions are a condition for, that alcohol dependence emerge, 3) that the socio-cultural conditions determine if you become an alcohol addict. Parallel to these views, and for the moment supposedly dominating, there are views which emphasize that alcoholism has a multifactorial etiology.

With a heterogeneous set of signals from the scientific world one could expect problems in determining the content in a daily-life understanding of causes of alcoholism. Notwithstanding the relation, which it is indicated previously must exist, the daily-life understandings have an "own-life" which render, that they are not immediate reflections of the formal theories, nor do they necessarily mirror the more or less subtle differences. Our idiosyncratic attitude towards the phenomenon alcoholism, as well as towards the more general condition constituted by "reasons to drink alcohol", is a result of a working together of our general view of man, our understanding of conditions for existence in society, general cultural and subcultural values and concrete life experiences. In our theoretical frame of understanding we would say that the *Alcohol Consumer Consciousness* would be the governing factor (Sabroe, 1989).

It is important in this connection not to forget the situational factor or the group perspective. Regardless of, that we as individuals most often appear with a relatively coherent horizon regarding certain matters, one can in relation to surveys etc. find results, which apparently express a discrepancy in the given answers about the same subject (Sabroe, 1984, p. 173). But precisely the situation in which the answer is given or to which it is "thought to belong", can be of decisive importance and determine seemingly contradictory responses.

It is the well-researched area of alcoholism mainly, which has been the foundation of the considerations above, but the subject of the presentation is not alcoholism, but "reasons for drinking". As already indicated one does not find the extensive literature which covers causes of alcoholism when the subject is "reasons for drinking". But related views can be found though, as for example by Room (1974), who deals with attitudes to alcohol and speaks of prevention, but whose considerations could nevertheless be reformulated in three "pictures": 1) Alcohol has become, through its existence in society, immensely attractive as stimulant, but at the same time must be regarded as dangerous for health, 2) Social interplay leads to conflict, of which alcohol is a culturally provided and obvious possibility of escape and hereby becomes destructive for behaviour, 3) Alcohol is relatively innocent, except for a very few especially predisposed individuals - unknown for what reason. Reformulated to "reasons to drink alcohol" this could be expressed: 1) Alcohol exists and we recognize its possibilities, and because it exists, we must have it. 2) Alcohol exists, and when we engage in certain (conflictual) social situations, we (in our culture) use alcohol. 3) Alcohol exists, and no problems are associated with it for the vast majority in society. As can be seen, such derived assumptions cannot directly be connected with the formal theories and they rather reflect their political/general foundation, as illustrated above.

3 Basis of data

Obviously, results being collected through an open formulated question of respectively to drink or not to drink alcohol, cannot isolated draw a picture of why people drink alcohol. Alcohol is interwoven with daily life in such a way in our society that a valid picture necessarily must draw on analyses of society, local area, group and individual level and furthermore include analyses of the way alcohol form part of the cultural history, its place in the actual historic situation and in the specific subcultural circumstances, which characterizes the investigated population. Creating the possibility that the respondents can express themselves freely in relation to the two questions, we have the chance to uncover an aspect of this complicated picture by taking the assertments of the single member of society as valid data.

The project group discussed, whether the data should be collected from closed questions/scales or from free responses. In accordance with the project's theoretical and methodological foundation which emphasized not to preformulate statements or answer-possibilities, but let the investigated define subject-areas, the latter possibility was chosen. In the survey the respondents were asked: "Give three reasons for drinking alcohol" and "Give three reasons for not drinking alcohol".

Surveys with open questions are not common, ordinarily the researchers will have selected five to ten "reasons" and either ask the respondent to put a mark against or to give priority to a certain amount or to come to a decision to all on a three to five sections scale (Miner & Ubago, 1987). From a research activity at the university of Athens - which employs the alcohol consumer consciousness concept as developed in our project - a survey exists (population 4,500), in which a question was formulated openly, but with the wording: "Mention three main reasons for drinking alcohol" (Madianou, 1988).

The open form appeared to be technically unproblematic, 88% responded to the request in this form. Analysing the data, it of course means a greater work on account of the extensive not presystematized amount of data. In the analysis a procedure was used in which two research-associates and a student-researcher read all the responses, which varied from single words to shorter sentences. On the background of this acquisition and through a "qualitative work-up" of the data, a series of themes was established, which stood out in the responses. There was a great accordance between the themes suggested by the three project-associates especially for the four-five main themes. For the minor prominent themes there were differences, but mostly expressing degrees of differentiation among the three evaluators. The advanced themes then were used systematically as criteria for statistical analyses.

4 Results

Great differences were found in the themes that were the prevailing for the two questions as expected. But for reasons as well to drink as not to drink there are four-five dominant themes. In table 1 and 2 are shown the frequencies for the two questions, the themes arranged in rank-order.

4.1 Reasons for drinking alcohol

For both sets of data the themes derived represent different spheres of life. For reasons to drink (table 1) the themes 2, 3 and 5 clearly express relations of social origin and maybe also 7 can be included, although individual conditions definitely are attached to the theme. The themes 1, 4, 6 and 8 are individually oriented on the other side, while theme 9 seems to be the result of a special interpretation of the question, in which the negative connotations, previously pointed out, have had their impact. Besides, the positive oriented themes dominate reasons to drink, only 1/8 of the population have chosen to formulate problem oriented themes. The social oriented themes are slightly predominant (43.1%) in relation to the individual oriented (38.3%); incidentally, the picture is in accordance with the data on which situations alcohol is used mainly: Home-life, the family gatherings and conviviality with friends do play the most important role (Sabroe & Rasmussen, 1993).

Table 1. Reasons for drinking alcohol (percentage)

THEMES	REASONS FOR DRINKING
1 Taste, relish	18.3
2 Family connection, conviviality	17.8
3 Relaxation, cosiness	16.4
4 Problems, stress, loneliness	10.8
5 Atmosphere, mood	8.9
6 Thirst	6.6
7 Food-accompany	3.1
8 Health (positive)	2.6
9 Habit, dependence	1.6
10 Various	1.6
11 No answer	12.4
Total	100.0 (N=1,754)

Results from investigations in other cultural settings can be drawn on in comparison. In the previously mentioned Greek survey the responses from a similar question were grouped in four dominant reasons (ranked): 1) Being with friends, 2) For enjoyment, 3) Setting atmosphere and 4) Accompanying food, followed - but clearly with less support - by reasons, which could be related to 5) Self confidence, overcome difficulties, anxiety etc. and 6) Curiosity (Madianou, 1989). Minor differences in the rank order of these reasons were found when related to age groups. In a major Spanish survey in which - as previously mentioned - fixed answer questions were used, the dominating reasons to drink alcohol were: 1) An excellent way to have feast, 2) It is the way to be with friends, 3) It is a good experience and 4) It is part of a good diet, the last reason clearly reflecting the Spanish origin of the data (Miner & Ubago, 1987).

4.2 Reasons for not drinking alcohol

In general, the responses to this question maybe could be labelled "risk considerations". In any case a pronounced result is that nearly 1/3 of the reasons for not drinking alcohol is related to health, and if driving, dependence, negative behavioral changes, work problems and social consequences are included as "risk related" more than 2/3 of the reasons will fall under a risk label. It is also characteristic that in their immediate appearance the themes on the whole represent individual-oriented reasons, even though social connections are clearly present.

Table 2. Reasons for not drinking alcohol (percentage)

THEMES	REASONS FOR DRINKING
1 Health (negatively)	31.6
2 Driving, traffic	17.1
3 Habit, dependence	8.6
4 Do not like it, taste (negatively)	6.2
5 Economy	5.8
6 Beliefs, faith	4.0
7 Personal consequences, hangover	3.7
8 Behavioral changes, aggression	2.8
9 Consequences for work	2.7
10 Social consequences	1.4
11 Sport	0.6
12 No answer	15.5
Total	100.0 (N=1,754)

Comparing with the Spanish survey previously mentioned the main reasons found here were: 1) Health, 2) Consequences for work, 3) Loss of control, 4) Dependence and 5) Unpleasant personal consequences (ibid., 1987). The Greek survey did not carry this question.

4.3 Group oriented reasons to drink alcohol

4.3.1. Sex
The general knowledge regarding patterns of drinking suggests differences in the priority of reasons to drink between men and women.

Table 3. Reasons for drinking in relation to sex (percentage)

| THEMES | SEX | |
	MEN (N=868)	WOMEN (N=886)
Taste, relish	20.1	16.5
Family connections, conviviality	17.5	18.2
Relaxation, cosiness	15.2	17.7
Problems, stress, loneliness	10.5	11.0
Atmosphere, mood	9.3	8.4
Thirst	10.7	2.5
Food-accompany	1.6	4.4
Health (positive)	1.6	3.6
Habit, dependence	1.3	1.8
Various	1.6	1.6
No answer	10.6	14.2
Total	100.0	100.0

The picture shown in the table is - not entirely unexpected, then - that men to a higher degree than women emphasize taste, relish and thirst while women choose relaxation, cosiness, food-accompany and health. Tradition and sexual roles seem to influence the responses.

4.2.2. Age
In relation to age one could expect differences in statements of reasons to drink also, supposedly with a clear discrepancy between younger and elder age groups. In table 4 are presented the themes which give significant differences ($p=<.001$).

Table 4. Reasons for drinking in relation to age (percentage)

THEMES	>20 (N=113)	20'ies (N=309)	30'ies (N=403)	40'ies (N=421)	50'ies (N=260)	60'ies (N=338)
Taste, relish	26.5	23.2	19.3	18.7	14.5	12.5
Family connections, conviviality	7.1	11.8	15.0	18.1	25.4	24.0
Relaxation, cosiness	14.2	19.6	20.1	19.0	14.5	8.9
Atmosphere, mood	21.2	11.1	7.5	10.1	4.7	6.2
Thirst	2.7	7.2	8.8	8.0	5.9	3.9
Health (positive)	0.9	2.6	1.8	1.8	4.3	3.9
Habit, dependence	3.5	1.6	2.0	1.8	1.2	0.3

The importance of taste, relish and atmosphere for the younger age groups is demonstrated clearly in the table; for the elder age groups family gatherings, conviviality and health are prevalent. It is noteworthy also (and predictable) that relaxation, cosiness and thirst are relatively often stated by the middle age groups.

4.3.2. Social groups

It appears from the data that for some themes there is a correlation between reasons to drink alcohol and social groups. In table 5 the themes are shown for which significant differences are present (p=<.01). For the rest of the themes there are smaller differences, not reaching a significant level.

Table 5. Reasons for not drinking alcohol in relation to social groups (percentage)

THEMES	SOCIAL GROUPS					
	GR. 1	GR. 2	GR. 3	GR. 4	GR. 5	REST GR.
	(N=86)	(N=119)	(N=439)	(N=503)	(N=57)	(N=550)
Taste, relish	36.0	21.6	21.8	16.0	14.7	3.5
Family connection, conviviality	8.1	21.1	18.6	19.4	15.1	22.8
Thirst	9.3	8.0	7.1	6.5	5.6	1.8
Problems, stress, loneliness	7.0	9.0	8.3	10.3	14.4	15.8

From the figures it is evident that the themes task and relish together with thirst are chosen by social group 1 (the upper strata) most often, while the theme problems to a higher degree is connected with social group 5. For these three themes there is an increasing, respectively decreasing tendency going from social group 1 to 5. Crucial is the heavy weight given by social group 1 to taste and relish.

The rest group represents respondents for whom insufficient data were present to place them in the social group stratification - established by the Danish Social Research Institute (SFI). This group is very large, one reason being that the variables the data collecting institution (AIM) used for this survey did not include all the background variables demanded to apply the SFI stratification in its fullest sense; the social stratification used is based on fewer variables. Another reason is that the share in the investigated population of pensioners, early retired, and "not in a working position" are relatively great and for these categories information which allows a precise placing in a social group often are lacking. This fact could lie behind the weighting of "Family connection, conviviality" by this group.

4.3.4 Income
It is obvious that income is related to social group - even if not directly. Nevertheless, the result will be given separately. In table 6 five themes are presented

for which clear differences turn up. Income is given as the actual figure by the respondents but is statistically grouped in three groups approximately of the same size.

Table 6. Reasons for drinking alcohol in relation to income (percentage)

| THEMES | INCOME | | |
	LOW (N=478)	MIDDLE (N=684)	HIGH (N=410)
Taste, relish	14.6	17.1	24.8
Family connection, conviviality	18.6	17.0	15.4
Relaxation, cosiness	11.2	20.1	18.4
Atmosphere, mood	10.8	8.6	7.6
Thirst	3.6	7.2	10.0

For the three overlapping themes from the social group data the tendency is the same. The differences are distinct with taste, relish, relaxation and thirst relatively more often chosen by the high income group, while conviviality, family gatherings and atmosphere, mood, are chosen by the low income group. The low-income group differs clearly from the other two by fewer, who state relaxation, cosiness.

4.3.5 Consumer groups
Reasons to drink could be expected to be related to own amount of consumption, anticipating differences especially between low and high consumer groups. For five of the themes such differences appear and are shown in table 7.

Table 7. Reasons for drinking alcohol in relation to consumer groups (percentage)

THEMES	0 - <1 (N=360)	1-6 PER WEEK (N=747)	7-13 PER WEEK (N=404)	14-20 PER WEEK (N=137)	>20 PER WEEK (N=105)
Taste, relish	9.2	18.2	23.8	21.7	24.8
Family connection, conviviality	21.2	17.9	17.5	17.4	6.7
Relaxation, cosiness	7.0	17.4	18.3	21.0	28.6
Problems, stress loneliness	15.9	9.8	9.0	9.4	8.6
Thirst	2.8	6.5	6.3	13.0	12.4

The results indicate marked differences, the group with a high consumption emphasizes taste, relish, relaxation, cosines and thirst, whereas the low consumption group chooses conviviality, family gatherings and "problems" relatively more often.

There are no significant differences between the consumption groups regarding reasons not to drink alcohol. But comparing the groups with lowest consumption and high consumption, two themes indicate differences. The high consumers to a higher degree state car driving (24% as against 18%) and the low consumer health (34% as against 28%). for the remaining themes no differences appear or the figures are so small that calculation will be meaningless.

5 Summing up and discussion

In alcohol research the question of reasons to drink, respectively not to drink alcohol, will always be central. It is obvious that optimal answers to questions like these only can be obtained from qualitative interviewing. In pilot-investigations leading up to the project of "The Danes' Alcohol Consumer Consciousness", qualitative interviewing has been undertaken including discussion reasons to drink or not to drink alcohol. From these interviews tendencies indicate an alcohol consumption behaviour that is anchored in family situations, conviviality with friends and other close social contact situations (Sabroe & Rasmussen, 1987a & b). On this background, a wish of a broader documentation emerged and given the opportunity to include alcohol questions in a survey on crisis-behaviour, it was decided to formulate two *open* questions of reasons to drink/not to drink alcohol. The aim was to collect immediate responses from a greater number of people in order to ascertain, if dominant relations would appear, if the responses to the two questions would originate from a common field of subjects (e.g. generally problem-oriented). It is obvious that through the phrasing of the questions the respondents could experience an appeal to answer in "positive" respectively "negative" terms. But with the subject of alcohol potentially being a loaded subject it could not be taken for granted that the responses unequivocally would be in positive or negative categories. In addition to this it was obvious that the category content would be of interest if the results should be employed for prevention purposes. An immediate statement of reasons to drink alcohol (not to drink alcohol) could be regarded as a behaviour indicator which - especially if coherent patterns appear - could form part of considerations regarding alcohol policy efforts.

The results of the analysis indicate that a series of themes can be identified, being more or less pronounced, when a representative population is asked to state their reasons for drinking/not drinking alcohol. The set of themes obtained through the analysis of the open responses turned out to be different for the two questions. Responses to the question of reasons for drinking alcohol were predominantly positively formulated and with social oriented themes being most manifest. Reasons for not drinking on the other hand provoke responses with mainly risk oriented overtones and mostly individual oriented.

These results are in accordance with results from research having a different content and method, but which nevertheless could be compared in a broad perspective. It is the expectancy and risk research, in which the interest has been the population's statements, experiences, regarding consequences of alcohol consumption (Southwich et al., 1981; Rohsenow, 1983; Critchlow, 1987; Hauge & Irgens-Jensen, 1990, and Goldman et al., 1991). These sources concurrent report that positive expectations to a much higher degree are stated than negative expectations when linked to own alcohol consumption. If consumption of alcohol is evaluated in a society perspective, one, on the contrary, finds it high on the risk scale.

When applying cross-analyses using different background variables, a picture of systematically increasing or decreasing distributions and significant differences for several of the themes appears. Thus, a picture presents itself which indicates, for reasons to drink, that:

1. *Taste, relish, atmosphere* and *thirst* as reasons to drink are more often stated by *men*, the *younger* age groups, the *upper social* groups, the *high income* groups and *heavy drinkers*.

2. *Family gathering* and *conviviality* are conversely more often chosen by *women*, in the *elder* age groups, the *lower social* groups and by the *low amount alcohol users*.

For a variable as *relaxation* the relations are ambiguous and for the rest of the variables the figures are too small to be used in a meaningful cross-analysis.

If a similar analysis is accomplished for *reasons not to drink*, relations are not found to the same extent. The relationships accentuated are health, driving and economy. *Women* and the *young* age groups more often choose health as a reason for not drinking alcohol. *Driving* is relatively more often the choice of *men*, *high income* groups and *heavy drinkers*, while *economy* is most common among the *eldest* and in the *high income group*.

The differences in the results regarding the two questions could be of importance in prevention, especially if considering the responses when grouped with regard to the average amount of alcohol drunken. What separates the consumer groups apparently are the positive reasons to drink alcohol rather than the negative stated reasons not to drink alcohol (risk views), and studying the reasons to drink alcohol we find an apparently coherent picture for the majority of the central variables. Discussion of either to employ general or specific *warnings* or to go for a *consumption-oriented understanding* - in preventive efforts - could be qualified through the application of the information and analyses presented above.

The positively formulated or consumer-oriented picture of alcohol drawn through the responses, seemingly, is in accordance with a Danish understanding - in the ascendant since Second World War - in which alcohol is regarded as a consumer goods. It is a view apparently established early in the process of socialization. In a pilot investigation at a school in the city of Aarhus, the results indicated that when 6-8 year old children (20 at all participated) were asked to make a drawing of a "person drinking alcohol", a "person not drinking alcohol" and of "children with adults drinking alcohol", the drawings of persons, who drank alcohol, were predominantly "positively imagined". No drawings had people from social marginal situations, but chiefly included common happy people or people with mild characteristics of intoxication. The vast majority of people who drank alcohol were men, however, only a single child drew a woman. Women dominated in drawings of persons who did not drink alcohol, on the other hand (Borregaard Nielsen & Sabroe, unpublished). The same "positive tendency" was present in the family drawings, and is to a certain degree contrary to similar analyses from other Scandinavian countries, for example Danielson (1982), who clearly indicates negative elements in drawings from children of the same age with skid-row persons more often present. If taking the responses of questions on alcohol (in general) from an accompanying survey, a tendency is found of more negative /dissociating responses among the younger school children (6-8 years) than of the elder (13-15 years), however.

It is evident that an alcohol consumer consciousness, of which the substance alcohol enters into positive connections (in its cognitive anchoring and emotional constraint), is a historical product. The alcohol consumer consciousness is not fixed or unalterable. It is the result of the individual's mutual relations with the surroundings, in which the economically, legally, general and specific culturally framing are important for its development. The individual alcohol user behaviour resulting herefrom also will be "historically determined" therefore, carrying along socially set conditions, but in its concrete amplification representing the individuals' elaboration of these conditions.

In the debate on prevention it has been claimed, that the knowledge regarding health related risk of heavy drinking is poor, maybe except the relation to liver cirrhosis. But the results presented above indicate, that at least an acknowledged general relation exists between alcohol and health in the population. But irrespective of, that this acknowledged relationship apparently (together with other risk factors) is an element of consciousness, a positive world of experience around alcohol is nevertheless present in the population, illustrated in the responses to the question on reasons to drink alcohol. This picture is supported by results from Rasmussen & Sabroe (1989) in which 76% (from a representative population of 2000) states, that alcohol negatively influences health, but well over 76% in the same survey express also that in general alcohol is a good in their life (only 9% state that it is generally an evil).

One could postulate that there is a contradiction in this picture. But on the one hand responses to survey questions etc. - as argumented p. 107 - must always be evaluated in relation to the situation they are thought belonging to, and "health" and "daily life" are not "merging concepts" necessarily. But in matter of explanation it could also be argued, that the two convictions of health risk and life-good exist "side by side" in the consciousness. An intervening variable, which with Schiøler (1987) could be named "cultural immunity", incurs and constitutes the individual behaviour, causing that the acknowledged risk of health "does not become a reality". Alcohol becomes a consumer-goods, which is used with thoughtfulness and unproblematic by the vast majority of the population. Through an appropriate daily alcohol behaviour the (acknowledged) health risk connected with alcohol is eliminated for the overall majority, and the experienced positive effects (especially as social lubricant and means of relish) obtain pregnancy and can be expressed in the statement that alcohol in general is a good in life.

In relation to prevention this raises a problem, when the goal of the preventive efforts is a reduction. For how does one communicate in reduction terms about a matter, which is not experienced as hostile in relation to the individual's health or social life? It is my opinion that choice of arguments with *insight character* (extended consciousness) and *not submissive character* (passive resignation) is important. In the terms of the project's frame of reference the aim must be to establish an *active alcohol consumer consciousness* (Sabroe, 1989).

An active alcohol consumer consciousness could be an essential preventive factor for a very substantial part of the population. But it is important that it does not become a pretext for doing nothing with the consequence of declaring oneself satisfied. It is obvious that a problem exists, which has to be solved through other "methods", when it is the case that Denmark has an unacceptably high per capita consumption. But, in particular, when we know that the consumption is marked lopsided, a lopsidedness indicating that 14-15% are drinking half the amount of the alcohol drunk in Denmark. This means that more than 400,000 above the age of 15 have a consumption at a level which at least potentially are being psychologically or somatically harmful and/or giving problems with their social functioning.

REFERENCES

Borregaard Nielsen, E. & Sabroe, K.-E. (1988) *Pilotprojekt om børns alkohol-bevidsthed*. Upubliceret rapport. (Pilot study on children alcohol consciousness).

Chritchlow Leigh, B. (1987). Beliefs about effects of alcohol on self and others. *Journal of Studies on Alcohol, 48*, 467-475.

Danielson, N. (1982) Kompletterande teckningsanalyser. I Nelson-Löftgren, I. *Barns forställninger om alkohol*. Stockholm. (Analysis of children's drawing of alcohol situations).

Edwards, G. & Grant, M. (1978) *Alcoholism*. London: Croom Helm.

Furnham, A. & Lowick, V. (1984) Lay theories on the causes of alcoholism. *Brit. Journ. Med. Psychology. 57*, 319-332.

Flensted-Nielsen, J. & Maack Evers, A. (1984) Alkoholisme. Særtryk *Månedsskrift for praktisk lægegerning*. 59-94. (Alcoholism).

Goldman, M., Brown, S.A., Christiansen, B.A. & Smith, G.T. (1991). Alcoholism and memory. *Psychological Bulletin, 110*, 137-146.

Hauge, R. & Irgens-Jensen, O. (1990). The experience of positive consequences of drinking in four Scandinavian countries. *British Journal of Addiction, 85*, 645-653.

Madianou, D. (1989) *Alcohol consumer consciousness. An anthropological approach*. Report to EEC Directorate General. Mimeo, 73 s.

Mandell, W. (1983) Types and phases of alcohol dependence illness. In Galander, M. *Recent developments in alcoholism. Vol. I*. New York: Plenum.

Mansell Pattison, E. & Kaufman, E. (1982) *Encyclopedic handbook of alcoholism*. New York: Gardiner Press.

Miner, M.G. & Ubago, J.G. (1987) *Community response to alcohol related problems*. Paper WHO Conference Lisboa, June. Mimeo, 30 p.

Ohlson, B.C. (1991). Instrumentell rationalitet eller populism. *Nordisk Alkohol Tidskrift*, I, *8*, 321-330. (Instrumental rationality or populism.)

Petersen, E., Dahlberg-Larsen, J., Goul Andersen, J., Sabroe, K.-E., Sommerlund, B. (1989) *De krisebevidste og ansvarsfulde danskere*. Århus: Psykologisk Institut. (The crisis conscious and responsible Danes).

Petersen, E., Sabroe, K.-E., Kristensen, O.S. (1987) *Danskernes tilværelse under krisen. Bd. I. Studier i krisens psykologiske virkninger*. Århus: Aarhus Universitetsforlag. (The Danes during the Crisis I. Studies in the psychological effects of the Crisis).

Petersen, E., Sabroe, K.-E., Sommerlund, B. (1987) *Danskernes tilværelse under krisen. Bd II. Studier i den plitisk-psykologiske udvikling 1982-86.* Århus: Aarhus Universitetsforlag. (The Danes during the Crisis II. Studies in the political-psychological development 1982-86).

Rasmussen, O. & Sabroe, K.-E. (1989) *Alcohol Consumer Consciousness. Survey data, frequency tables.* Århus: Psykologisk Institut.

Rohsenow, D.J. (1983). Drinking habits and expectancies about alcohol's effects for self and others. *Journal of Consulting and Clinical Psychology, 51,* 752-756.

Room, R. (1974) Govering images and the prevention of alcohol problems. *Preventive Medicine, 3,* 11-23.

Sabroe, K.-E. (1984) *Socialpsykologi. Forståelsesrammer og begreber.* København: Akademisk Forlag. (Social Psychology. Frames of understanding and concepts).

Sabroe, K.-E. (1989) Alcohol Consumer Consciousness. A social psychological perspective. *Proceedings 35th ICAA, vol. IV,* Oslo: National Directorate for the Prevention of Alcohol and Drug Problems. 1-21.

Sabroe, K.-E. & Rasmussen, O. (1987a). Forprojektrapport. Upubliceret manus. (Pilot study, unpublished).

Sabroe, K.-E. & Rasmussen, O. (1987b). Progress report II. Aarhus: Institute of Psychology. Mimeo, 17 p.

Sabroe, K.-E. & Rasmussen, O. (1993). *Alkohol Forbruger Bevidsthed* (in print). Alcohol Consumer Consciousness).

Schiøler, P. (1987) *Cultural immunity.* Paper at Symposium. University of Erasmus, Rotterdam. Jan., mimeo, 10 p.

Southwick, L., Steele, C., Marlatt, A. & Lindell, M. (1981). Alcohol related expectancies. *Journal of Consulting and Clinical Psychology, 49,* 713-721.

7.

ALCOHOL, LOW PRICE, AVAILABILITY - INCREASED CONSUMPTION?

1. Introduction

The threesome of *control, restricted availability* and *price policy* is often advanced as effective means of prevention in the debate on alcohol policy. Grant (1985) argued for example that cross-national experiences seem to support that the application of one or more of these three factors will result in reduction of consumption. The arguments frequently are based on analyses of introduction or abolishment of the three kinds of initiatives in a national or regional connection. In this paper presenting the problem will be reversed in a way. The question will be raised, if an existing situation with low price on alcohol combined with a relatively easy availability to this alcohol for a given population will lead to a higher consumption, compared with the consumption of other populations in the same culture group.

1.1. The border problem

Denmark and Germany have a 50 km border between Jutland and Schleswig-Holstein. Both countries are members of the EU, but there is a considerable difference between prices on alcohol in the two countries, nevertheless. Returning from a drive across the border (the nearest greater city in Germany being less than five km's away) a Danish citizen above the age of 17 can take home *five* litres of wine, *three* litres of fortified wine and *ten* litres of beer according to the rules being in force during recent years. Identical commodities would amount to about 500 Dkr. (equal to 83 $) purchased in Denmark, being table wines, ordi

[1] Cand.psych. Palle Schriver with assistance from associate professor, cand.scient. Bo Sommerlund, has established the statistical models and Palle Schriver has performed the statistical analyses.

nary aperitifs or inexpensive sherries/ports and normal beers. In Germany identical goods could be bought for about 230 Dkr. (equal to 38 $).[2]

It is of no surprise, then, that Bygvraa et al. (1987) have been able to show a substantial import of alcohol over the Danish-German border by Danish citizens. It is calculated that a person living within a distance of 50 km from the border purchases 68% of his/her alcohol in Germany, if the distance is 50-125 km the percentage is 35 and above 125 km it is 10-15% (ibid.). An interesting question is, if the low price alcohol and the relatively easy availability will result in an increased consumption for the 50 km-region (less than one hour's drive from the nearest cities in Germany). Besides purchasing the major amount of his/her alcohol in Germany, other advantages can be obtained, electrical, electronic and several other articles are also cheaper, and petrol is up to 2 Dkr. (equal to 0.35 $) lower than in Denmark. The incentives to go shopping in Germany thus are strong and as already mentioned above, in the international debate on alcohol policy it has generally been claimed that low price and easy accessibility will lead to an increased consumption of alcohol.

2. Alcohol consumption region-distributed

Collection of data for a major survey using telephone interviewing and comprising 2000 participants (Sabroe, 1988; Rasmussen & Sabroe, 1990), provided the opportunity to calculate the average consumption (number of drinks per week) for regions in Jutland. The division of Jutland into regions could be according to the counties of (from South to North) South Jutland, Ribe, Vejle, Aarhus, Ringkøbing, Viborg and North Jutland, but sub-division of the areas is possible and will be applied in the analyses. The population of the analysis is a part-population from a country-sample and not constructed, thus, with the specific purpose of elucidating the border-trade problems. Vejle County constitutes a special area of analysis in the project connection and is stronger represented (equal to a 0.3% sample) as a subpopulation therefore than the other counties (equal to a 0.02% sample). This condition should be of minor importance, however, when using rank-order analyses, as a statistical foundation for the argumentation.

---

[2] All figures are, if not otherwise identified, valid for the situation in late 1991. From January 1993 the situation has changed. The difference in petrol price no longer exists, and the difference in alcohol prices is reduced. On the other hand, the amount allowed to bring back from a one-day crossing of the border has, due to harmonization of EU rules, been greatly increased. The effect of this change has not been sufficiently elucidated, yet.

In the survey several measures of alcohol consumption are used. For this article
"stated average number of drinks per week" is chosen. Analyses have also been
carried out in relation to *"consumption yesterday"* and *"consumption of the week"*
(measured on the basis of daily specifications), but these analyses have not
changed the conclusions based on the measures of weekly average of drinks.

3. Average consumption and border-distance

In order to find a suitable model for statistical analysis, several have been tried. One major demand was that it should be able to make an allowance for the fact, that the samples were so relatively small (50-60 persons). If for example a single person with an extremely high consumption were part of the sample, the consumption distribution could be pulled askew. Although a basis could be found for a concluding argumentation in the immediate statements of an average consumption, it was decided to compensate for the skewness which comes about in relation to normal averages, as a result of the above mentioned, and employ a rank-order test.

Describing the regional differences in consumption-statements a Kruskal-Walis one-way test is employed, while distances to the border are described through Spearman-correlations. The distances to the border are measured for each of the municipalities in the Vejle County (due to the special position of this county in the investigation) and estimated for the remainder regions on the basis of the centre of gravity of the population in the region.

The result of the analyses is that *no* general connection can be documented between border distance and the consumption statements from the total population of 1392 persons. A correlation of .000 is found between border distance and statements of yesterdays consumption, which is the applied measure of consumption giving the greatest declarations of drinks consumed per person. Further the analysis indicated that a possible effect of border trade ought to appear most clearly in the statements of average weekly consumption, which is the measure most sensitive to small differences between low-amount consumers. This measure of consumption produces a faint correlation ($r = -.056$) with border distance, but at the same time there is a very high significant difference between regions ($p < .004$).

In table 1 is illustrated a possible effect on the average weekly consumption from border trade. The individuals in the different regions are placed on a scale of distance to the border and on a logarithmic scale for average consumption, with 0 being one drink per week, and each whole interval equivalent to an increase of 100%.

Table 1. Average consumption and border distance

Number of drinks per week		Number of persons	Distance to the border (region average)									
log2	scale	total	30	80	90	100	110	130	140	150	200	280
	-4	5		1			1				1	2
-3.9	- -3	11			1		5	1	2		1	1
-2.9	- -2	19	1	2			2	2	6	1	4	1
-1.9	- -1	29	2	6	5		2	2	3	1	3	5
-0.9	- 0	141	4	19	10	6	28	11	36	4	13	10
0.1	- 1	173	8	22	14	2	34	12	34	4	25	18
1.1	- 2	238	11	33	15	7	55	11	43	1	39	23
2.1	- 3	287	14	47	19	13	61	14	60	5	40	14
3.1	- 4	197	2	31	23	3	44	8	36	4	35	11
4.1	- 5	76	5	8	6	2	20	4	16		12	3
5.1	- 6	14	1	2	1	1	3		2		4	
6.1	- 7	3					1		2			
7.1	- 8	2							1		1	
Number of consumers		1195	48	171	94	34	256	65	241	20	178	88
Average		6.61	6.2	6.2	6.4	6.3	6.8	4.7	7.5	4.1	7..9	4.3
Average (log2)		1.71	1.7	1.8	1.8	2.0	1.8	1.3	1.7	1.0	1.9	1.1
No consumption		(7%)	4%	7%	6%	3%	5%	17%	6%	13%	10%	6%
Total		1285	50	183	100	35	269	78	256	23	197	94
Average (total)		6.15	6.0	5.8	6.0	6.1	6.4	3.9	7.1	3.5	7.2	4.1

The table indicates that the stated average consumption exceeds seven drinks per week in the two areas 140 and 200 km from the border, only . In the Southern and the Northern part of Jutland the same amount of drinks per week is stated. This is due to the fact that two persons stating the very high consumption of more than 128 drinks per week both live north of the median, and the correlation between the 1195 persons' distance to the border and placement on the logarithmic scale is similar to the nonparametric correlation for all 1285 persons (r = -.058; p = .047 unilateral estimation).

This should immediately result in an average scale value of 2.01 close to the border and a fall of .0019 per kilometre, one leave the border. Over a distance of 100 km the fall in the average consumption should be of about 13%. In the table we see that the scale averages gradually *rise* over the first 100 km, however. The line of regression is out of step with the conditions in that part of Jutland, thus, in which differences in border trade involve a considerable part of the population. The conclusion is, therefore, that there is a significant difference between regions, but *nothing indicates* that easy accessibility of low-priced alcohol in the southern regions is a major cause of these registered differences.

Two regions separate themselves from the others having a significantly lower consumption, one is a region about 150 km from the border, the other the most northern 100 km of Jutland. The latter region was in an exceptional position already in the preliminary analyses, and the region maintains the position as the relatively lowest ranked region - with regard to consumption - in analyses employing all biographical and social variables.

Supplementary analyses, including the stated *rate of inebriation,* do not support a hypothesis of regional (distance related) differences. This is interesting as the "way of shopping" could be decisive for how easy it is for the single consumer to estimate his/her average consumption, but the way of shopping would probably not influence the consumer estimates of the frequency of inebriation.

One condition worrying all investigators using survey data is a relatively great underreporting (40-60%) of consumption in relation to the national statistics of alcohol sold. If a systematic connection between underreporting and "way of shopping" could be assumed, we might have the explanation of not finding a general relation between estimates of consumption and border distance. Two hypotheses about a relation between underreporting and "way of shopping" shall shortly be commented.

One hypothesis is that a person generally making large-scale purchases (in casu in Germany) could have greater difficulty in estimating his/her average consumption (in weekly terms) on account of fewer number of points of reference than a person, for whom the purchases to a higher degree follow a consumption-cadence. We do not have specific data to elucidate the hypothesis, but we have demonstrated that no relationship are found between frequency of inebriation and border distance, and the hypothesis about large-scale purchases presumably cannot be related to the estimates of frequency of inebriation. There are, for that reason, circumstances (indirectly) indicating, that the hypothesis cannot be upheld of *large-scale purchases accounting for the non-existent relation consumption-border distance.*

The other hypothesis suggests that the single consumer to a greater degree controls his/her expenditure of commodities regarded as relatively expensive than commodities, which are purchable at low price. A higher degree of awareness of the consumption therefore ought to exist in areas with a longer distance to the border.

Nor in this case have we the possibility to test the hypothesis directly, but the relationship can be elucidated through an analysis involving a variable, which we have named *report-fall*. Report-fall is calculated as the difference between the stated consumption the two week-days nearest and the two farthest away in a period of seven days backwards from "yesterday" (week-ends are excluded due to their special status as regards consumption). Report-fall is a variable thus only possible to calculate for persons stating a consumption of week-days within the last week. In the survey participants were asked for the consumption for seven consecutive days backwards, among other consumption questions, and the last time when alcohol had been consumed, also.

Regarding the persons of whom a report-fall could be calculated, 45% were "in balance" or had a slight increase across the week, while 55% reported the highest consumption during the two nearest week-days, demonstrating a "report-fall", thus. The 45% who displayed "constancy" could be expected to have a better knowledge of their consumption than the 55% who presents a "fall".

As a group, the "constants" are characterized with a higher average consumption and a higher degree of balance between week-day and week-end consumption than the "fall" group. It is not possible to demonstrate any connection between the variable report-fall and border distance though. Nor does household-income show any relationship with report-fall.

Further analyses show that report-fall and its connection with consumption statements are not merely a question of having firm habits for consumption of alcohol. In a later publication evidence will be given supporting the fact that report-fall mirrors the consumer's awareness towards own consumption and therefore can have a control-function.

A postulate, which could be advanced with some caution, is that *if* report-fall can be regarded as a manifestation of underreporting (expressed through oblivion) and *if* the consumption on week-days can be considered as relatively constant, *underreporting* seems to be greatest among the low-amount consumers.

4. Biographic variables, consumption and border distance

Using the traditional variables of sex, age, place of residence (urban-rural) and education in a cross-analysis, no indication of a connection between consumption and border distance appears. For the variable household-income there seems to be a relation - higher consumption in the border region - for the medium range income (200-300.000 Dkr., equal to 33-50.000 $), as shown in table 2.

Table 2: Household-income, consumption and border distance (Household-income 200.000-300.000)

Distance (km)	Average consumption (log 2)	Number
30	8.9	10
80	6.3	29
90	9.1	24
100	5.7	6
110	5.5	52
130	5.7	12
140	5.3	51
150	2.3	9
200	4.8	40
280	4.3	18
Total	5.7	251

p = .001

For household-incomes *below* 200.000 Dkr. and *above* 300.000 Dkr., *no* significant differences are found.

5. Average consumption, attitudes and border distance

Taking the attitude questions used in the survey an analysis was carried out involving those of: 1) Alcohol is generally a good, 2) Alcohol is generally an evil, 3) Alcohol is good for health, 4) Alcohol is bad for health. In none of these cases was found a relation to border distance.

6. Summing up and discussion

A detailed set of analyses employing general calculation of averages, rank-order tests and log 2 distributions *do not support a hypothesis assuming that relatively easy availability of low price alcohol for a group of consumers in a specific region will result in a consumption higher than average* in the greater national area, of which the region is a part. The conditional qualifications are that this consumption is registered in April-May 1989 - and alcohol is rather expensive in the home region due to a high taxation of spirits.

Nor indicates a split-up into subpopulations (according to sex, age, education, place of residence) a connection between consumption and border-distance. The inclusion of the variable report-fall also fails to prove a relationship with border-distance and consumption. One exception is household-income though. A division of the population into a low income (<199.999 Dkr.) a medium income (200.000-299.999 Dkr.) and a high income (>300.000) gives no support for a consumption - border distance relationship for the low income and high income groups. But for the *medium income* group one finds a connection with a higher consumption, when living relatively close to the border. Understanding this relation the following rough outline could be considered:

Low income group. The group is tied up economically, and disposition-opportunities are not present as regards large-scale purchases (which would supposedly be the motivation for investing in the longer drive) especially not, if the purchases are relatively luxury oriented as wine and fortified wine. The potential for increase of consumption is therefore not present.

High income group. This group has the economic means for making large-scale purchases, but having no economic incentives to take "the trouble" of the longer transport, the unfamiliar conditions of shopping etc. A potential increase of consumption will be relatively independent of distance to the border, therefore.

Medium income group. This group has to act economically, but is in a position of certain possibilities of disposition. For this group it could pay off to consider large-scale purchases in Germany. At the same time it could be expected, that quite many of his group are in a process of changing life style in the direction of greater enjoyment of life goods, including new drinking habits (increased wine consumption). It is a possibility, furthermore, that this happens as a supplementing and not a replacement of a previous drink pattern and give reasons to the demonstrated connection, thus.

An interesting question could be in relation to the *not-established* relation between easy availability to low price alcohol and increased consumption, if the relatively high per capita consumption in Denmark played a role. It is obvious that in the border area one buys the major part of the consumed alcohol in Germany, but regarding level of consumption a "balance" maybe has been attained which exceeded would result in a changed (more inappropriate) style of life. Culturally determined "preventive factors" therefore intervene and "block" a potential increase of consumption.

Supplementary analyses, recording the percentage in the different regions *drinking above the country average*, do not indicate a connection between border distance and percentage of heavy drinkers. On the contrary the counties of South Jutland and North Jutland have a significantly *lower* percentage of drinkers with an above average consumption. For the border area there seems to exist a greater spreading across the consumption groups (as measured by number of drinks per week) than in the Mid- and Western Jutland counties.

As a final remark it is important to call attention to the fact that the survey populations in the different regions are relatively small, except for Vejle County. This is a problem when division in relation to background variables is carried out. Compensation is attempted, employing statistical analyses (rank order tests) through which are reduced the implications of this. But a decisive factor bringing importance to the results is the consistency with which the data present themselves across the single variables.

References

Bygvraa, Susanne et al. (1987) *Den dansk-tyske grænsehandel.* Åbenrå: Institut for Grænseforskning. (The Danish-German Border Trade).

Grant, M. (1985) *Alcohol Politics.* Copenhagen: WHO Regional Publications, *no. 18.*

Rasmussen, O. & Sabroe, K.-E. (1989) Frequency tables. Aarhus: Institute of Psychology.

Sabroe, K.-E. (1988) Alcohol Consumer Consciousness. A social psychological perspective on alcohol. Oslo: National Directorate for the Prevention of Alcohol and Drug Problems. Proceedings 35th 1CAA, vol. IV, 1-21.

8.

THERAPIST CONSCIOUSNESS

THERAPIST CONSCIOUSNESS[1]

1. INTRODUCTION

The aim of the project "Alcohol Consumer Consciousness" is to obtain knowledge of how the individual - and in a further sense also how social groups or even the Danes "as a nation" - reacts towards the substance alcohol as a subject in social life and to consumption of alcohol. This aim we try to obtain as well through qualitative (extensive) interviewing as through quantitative (survey) techniques.

One extension of the project has been to undertake a pilot project aimed at an agency investigation. In accordance with the way of work in the project a theoretical understanding was elaborated before the empirical phase was launched, in this case a foundation for what we termed a "therapist consciousness" was a first task. The concept was developed in agreement with the theoretical basis of the Alcohol Consumer Consciousness concept (Sabroe, 1989), which means that social psychological and cognitive theory has played a major part.

2. EVERYDAY CONSCIOUSNESS AND PROFESSIONAL CONSCIOUSNESS

In his existence in daily life man is presented with a variety of information. This information is processed and organized in a way which gives man the possibility of interacting with his material and social surroundings. The resulting behaviour reflects how man perceives himself and his/her surroundings, and it is based on a knowledge, which all humans to a greater or lesser extent are in the possession of within a given society.

---

[1] This paper is based on a student research project carried out by stud.psych. Charlotte Bang and stud.psych. Charlotte Flydtkjær under the supervision of associate professor Knud-Erik Sabroe. The report of the project is of 170 pages and classified as confidential. For part of the article a draft form in Danish was made by Charlotte Bang. Knud-Erik Sabroe has extended the article and written it in its final English.

For subgroups there also exists an amount of knowledge within any society which is crucial for the behaviour in the situations specific for the subgroups. In order to come to an understanding of the professionals and other workers in client contact within the alcohol area, we coined the concept *therapist consciousness*. The concept of therapist consciousness is at the theoretical level divided into "everyday consciousness" and "professional consciousness", respectively.

The everyday consciousness must be understood in terms of the individual's experiences in the everyday world. The everyday world could be defined as the intersubjective world, which is experienced within and also from the point of view what Husserl terms the "natural attitude" (Schutz, 1975).

One could say that the everyday consciousness expresses itself through the knowledge, which the person possesses, and which at the same time is a "common possession" in the population. It is a common knowledge which is a "central content" of the consciousness acknowledged or at least potentially recognizable by the population in general. It is expressed through and interpreted within the framework of our collective social schemes of interpretation (Ibid.).

The professional consciousness, which in practice obviously cannot be separated from the everyday consciousness, primarily is conceived as the therapist's more specific experiences in relation to alcohol treatment. Besides the experiences from treatment it is important to consider the influence on the professional consciousness deriving from the physical and structural frames within which the alcohol-therapists works.

One could say that the professional consciousness first and foremost finds its expression in the workday through the actual job performance, and with regard to the interview situation the professional consciousness will find expression through the occupation related knowledge and through the job-experiences, which each of the therapists communicates.

This more specific knowledge on the one hand includes the indirect knowledge about alcohol treatment derived from teachers , colleagues, clients etc. and on the other hand the more direct knowledge constituted through personal experiences, acquired eo ipso the performance of the alcohol treatment job. The two life spheres of the therapist's everyday consciousness and professional consciousness are analytical divisions only and they of course are integrated parts of the individual's reality of life.

An operationalization of the concept of the "therapist consciousness" will imply, therefore, an analysis of how the content of the "therapist consciousness" is constituted within the therapist's above mentioned reality spheres. For this purpose we have drawn from the "Knowledge Sociology" and its insights in how common sense knowledge is constituted in the intersubjective everyday reality, and comprehension of how knowledge is socially distributed - in this context with regard to the professional expert-knowledge of the therapist (Berger & Luckmann, 1976).

3. THE CHARACTERISTICS OF THE ALCOHOL-THERAPIST'S JOB

When we use the term therapist in the coming, it is to be understood in a very broad sense, including "all" the groups which during an alcoholic career get into contact with the person. In the present pilot investigation we have interviewed two persons, thus, from each of the following groups: Psychiatric hospitals, general practitioners, alcohol treatment institutions, public assistance offices and police.

The pilot project is documented in a report of 170 pages (in Danish) which because of its content of personal information is classified confidential.

3.1. The therapist's adaptations-mechanisms.

As no absolute norms exist or what is *normal* nor for what is meant by *health*, it implies that the goals in alcohol treatment often appear as diffuse to the therapist. On account of problems with a positive value-oriented definition of these concepts, one often resorts to either quantative (statistical) definitions or negative demarcations. We do not follow up on this problem, but among other ways "of adapting" we will in this connection pay special attention to one way of the therapist's coping with the uncertainties and confusions in his job, which we call "*ideologizing*" (Herskin, 1980).

Values and norms are implicit with every form of choosing goal and method. These values and norms often will constitute an ideology superimposed on the methodology and theory of treatment, and hereby strengthen the adoption to the chosen process of dealing with clients, and the causes supposed to have brought them into their client situation. But an "ideology" is often short lived, though it spontaneously provokes excitement and engagement, and new ideologies readily present themselves, often first after a period of fall in enthusiasm, though.

Another widespread reason why enthusiasm falls is that there often is an experience of a lack of unambiguous and visible treatment results, especially when the therapist has used every effort and has chosen the method which to him seem to be the optimal method. The consequence from these "ups and downs" can be, that stable periods never come into existence, and that the treatment system therefore never functions with a maximum effectiveness.

Herskin (Ibid.) calls attention to the situation, that although the single treatment system as a whole appears to be characterized by the same form of ideologization, it is often only some of the members in the team that *internalize* the ideology, the rest of the group are merely sympathizers. This group can feel a pressure to practice the ideology, however, or they maybe feel attracted to the ideology by the actual attitudes, because of an identification with the persons who have internalized the ideology.

An ideology-oriented treatment system or an ideology-oriented therapist is motivated for carrying out his job tasks, obviously. The motivation can partly be found in the infectious enthusiasm, and partly in the high degree of community feeling participating in "realization" of the ideology. But the greatest impact might come from the fact that through the ideology is removed a great part of the uncertainties involved in the treatment situation.

Another important aspect for the professional alcohol-therapist is his task to help the client changing his life situation, of course. To do this a therapist is required to adopt a perspective differing from that of the client: an objectifying, rational engagement in the client and his/her situation. Not to do this would maintain the therapist in as powerless a situation as that of the client regarding the obtaining of the required change. Here is a risk that the therapist can get too *technically* involved in the client, however, and loose the personal empathic engagement which is an important aspect of any therapy at least to a psychologist. If the therapist becomes too technically oriented there is a risk that his/her actings and initiatives will be too heavily based on predetermined, fixed strategies. Expert knowledge with a character of rule of thumb will dominate in an inappropriate extent coupling client and actual (as well as historic) situations into fixed causal relationship. At least to this project group a personally and actionwise involvement in the client is important.

4.   THERAPIST CONSCIOUSNESS

The subject "therapist consciousness" have been defined in accordance with the theoretical foundations of the project (Sabroe, 1989). Besides the demographic variables we find that the aspects of treatment, experience, ethics, job performance, structural and material job conditions, team work and personal relation to alcohol is central in the definition and important to understand the actual therapist's consciousness. These aspects at the same time will be used as anchorpoints in the interview guide.

It is obvious that *age* constitute an important category because both secondary and tertiary socialization is age dependent (Sabroe, 1984), but it is to a high degree tied up with *sex* due to the social differences in male and female socialization.

The therapist's specific *education* and *number of years working with alcohol treatment system* was considered important categories also. It became evident in the preliminary interviews previous to the pilot project that the therapist consciousness to a high degree seemed determined by the kind and extent of formal education. It also was supported that the choice of *working place,* and the *period* the therapist has been dealing with alcohol problems was a correct one.

Treatment was an evident category, and through description of attitude towards *abuse of alcohol* and by way of describing *methods* and *goal-setting* for intervention a further important aspect of the therapist's consciousness was included.

Of importance is the therapist's *cognitive style* moreover, how he has *acquired his knowledge,* how he *applies this and acquired skills,* and how the therapist *finds, that his knowledge influences his attitudes towards alcohol problems.*

Essential in the therapist consciousness is the *understanding of own role in the client/therapist situation.* Personal experiences as well as *appraisal of how professional knowledge and skills can be applied* in the daily work is central of this aspect.

Ideological foundations of the therapists' job performance, reflections made on the role (prescriptive attitudes and acting) has been found definite in determining the therapist's consciousness and has been termed *meta-consciousness*. Further was implicated the experience of *structural* and *material working conditions,* the experience of and ideals for *team work*.

Finally the therapist's *personal relation* to the substance alcohol and to alcohol consumption was taken up as constituting the "therapist consciousness", supplemented with his attitudes towards the function of alcohol in society and of the dealing with alcohol related problems in society.

In overview the elements defining the concept "therapist consciousness" as used in this investigation is as follows :

DEMOGRAPHIC VARIABLES :
- age
- sex
- education
- number of years as alcohol therapist

TREATMENT
- attitude toward alcohol abuse
- choice of treatment method
- choice of treatment goals
- practising method and goal setting

PERSONAL EXPERIENCE
- own role in the client/therapist situation
- estimation of professional background in the job

META CONSCIOUSNESS
- ethics
- proper/defensible job performance

STRUCTURAL AND MATERIAL JOB CONDITIONS
- possibilities and limits in job performance
TEAMWORK
- internal teamwork
- external teamwork

PERSONAL RELATIONS TO ALCOHOL
- the functions of alcohol in society and for the individual
- own alcohol consumption patterns
- society and alcohol related problems

5.   RESEARCH METHOD

The aim of the pilot project was to carry out a qualitative study of "therapist consciousness". In the theoretical delimitation of the concept are as indicated above
found important traits and qualities of the common human, and social practice
and more specific characteristics features of the treatment job are drawn upon.

The elaboration of scientific explanation and description build upon a selection
and systematization of the material reality in question, which is concurrent for
how the investigated phenomenon appears.

Theoretically the conceptualization of "therapist consciousness" is essential. For
empirical investigation the concept is translated into operational constructs. The
research model developed aims at obtaining an understanding of the therapists'
psychological reality, and it aims at describing the qualities and states, which
indicate how the conception of the "therapist consciousness" can be reflected.

If the (theoretically founded) research model is accepted as valid - that the present interviews reflect what is intended, namely the "therapist's consciousness" -
then the methodological problem onwards consists of deciding on sufficient adequate methods of analysis, interpretation and mediation/description. In this in-
terpretation- and description-process a danger arises with regard to not reproduc-
ing the consciousness of the therapists, in the meaning universe of the therapist.

Schutz (1975) makes a distinction between a common sense and a scientific
construction of mental subjects. An inevitable human tendency to mix up a
common sense and scientific mode of thinking will occur, when we as researchers want to investigate the concept of "therapist consciousness" - during the interviewing and in the process of analysing and interpretation both. As far as
possible we have tried to be aware explicit of such an influence from our common sense constructions in our interpretation of the data.

5.1   The interview as a research method

Kvale (1979) describes the research interview as a method which intends to obtain qualitative descriptions of the interviewed person's life sphere with an eye
on interpreting the meaning in the phenomena in question. The method for this -
the qualitative method - can be defined as aiming at finding the qualities which

characterize a given phenomenon, at the same time making you able qualitatively to distinguish this phenomenon from others (Eneroth, 1984).

The qualitative method evidently is based on a certain understanding of reality: on the one hand an overall picture of the world and the phenomena in this world, and on the other hand a subject-subject relationship between the researcher and his subject-matter of research.

From the point of view that each quality of a given phenomenon or concept is looked upon as an aspect of the entirety each expression of the phenomenon is considered a concrete expression of it. You let - in the qualitative method - a few examples of a given phenomenon represent this phenomenon. Each of the qualities you find, by studying a few examples of a phenomenon, should be placed in an inner conjunction with the phenomenon as a whole therefore.

The qualitative research interview is not only an open and reciprocal conversation, but a conversation where the interviewer wants something from the interviewee in accordance with the purpose of the investigation. Both the interviewer and the interviewee will be in an interpreting position in the interview situation, and will react to what is said both. The interviewer is "co-creator" of the data through this interaction. In the analysis process the interpretation of the data-material will be based to a great extent on the impressions from and the familiarizing with the interview process. In this process the researcher's subjectivity will influence the interpretation of the content of the meaning in each of the interviews.

6. PRELIMINARY - RESULTS

The pilot investigation of the therapist consciousness, including ten alcohol-treatment employees in Vejle County suggests that differences exist with regard to the elements included in the concept theoretically. It seems as if the therapists experience their role in different ways, and these differences seem to a great extent derivable from distinctions in the specific function as regards the job, which again often is tied to a specific educational background (professional knowledge).

Some therapists signify that their formal education is of the greatest importance in performing their therapist role. These therapists often have a frequent and close contact to the clients, and point out, that their function is of a *professional* therapeutic character. The remaining therapists find to a higher degree that their common sense knowledge is of importance acquired through daily experiences in practising the therapist role. We find that we can identify the tendency that the more professional knowledge included in the alcohol-treatment work, the more the therapist is conscious of how the role context he enters can influence the treatment. The variations appearing among the interviewed therapists regarding attitudes towards the function of alcohol, the complexity of causes of alcohol abuse and the abuser as a type of person likewise seems to be related to the therapist's educational background for and job function in the alcohol-treatment.

These variations more deal with the extent to which the description of the mentioned topics are amplified and varied than with really differences as regards attitudes. We have tried to look for the *meaning* within the data obtained from each of the therapists. We have uncovered a relatively concordant understanding regarding the view of man that governs the attitudes towards and thinking of causes to abuse of alcohol among all the interviewees. But this superior agreement - regarding man as self-responsible and abuse as multifactorial caused - does not result in concordant understandings of method and goal in the treatment.

The treatment method is chosen by each of the therapists in accordance with the client's peculiarity and situation, founded on the therapist's professional (or eventually common sense) knowledge about the given problem. The "professional knowledge" is closely connected with educational and theoretically knowledge. "Common sense knowledge" on the other hand often is applied when the therapist has no formal (higher educational level) training. A general method of treatment across these differences seems to be use of the therapeutic dialogue or therapeutic group sessions, however.

Differences were present with regard to whom the therapists involved in a treatment sequence and when. This varies to a high degree with the therapist's understanding of alcohol abuse, the actual abuser and his social anamnesis and eventual progress within the social system. From a superior point of view it though seemed as if the therapists when choosing their treatment goals and methodology - as already stated above - leaned heavily on their specific educational background or in lack of formal education on common sense and concrete work experiences. In this way the same "type of client" often was treated differently.

In spite of the indicated importance of the education in the process of treatment you cannot point to a merging with regards to this between identically educated therapists across the alcohol-treatment agencies. It seemed as if a joint defining takes place across the educational differences of treatment method and of the particular goal setting for each client within a single agency. This collective defining is found to be the main factor behind the satisfactory teamwork experienced in general among the ten therapists regarding their own workplace.

The co-operation between the different alcohol-treatment agencies is estimated as unsatisfactory partly because of hindrances in the structure of the general treatment system, and partly because there are differences concerning methods and goals between the agencies. The factors, which are estimated as influencing the external co-operation positively - collegiate sympathy and concordance with regard to attitude - are the factors whose presence constitute a quite satisfactory internal teamwork in the single workplace.

In a wider perspective we could imagine, that the therapists were made aware of the relations we have found in the pilot project concerning the in- and external team-work. In the investigated part of alcohol-treatment system one could benefit from the experiences derived from the internal teamwork, concerning factors underlying a satisfactory teamwork, in the way that one in the external teamwork could attempt to work out concordance concerning method and goal in alcohol-treatment. A higher degree of identical norms regarding the treatment as well as increased personal and professional mutual acquaintance could affect the experienced impenetrability of the structure of the treatment system furthermore and establish a higher degree of clearness and transparency.

7.   FINAL REMARKS

The pilot project raised some important questions with regard to the psychological aspects of the "therapist consciousness". We did not reach any quantitative presentation of a consciousness scale in this pilot investigation, and we do not expect to be able to. It is our intent to try to establish a "typology", however, based on an "active - passive continuum" rather than on a "high - low". But this demands further investigations and further theoretical work. The pilot project in a way raised more questions than it answered, and one important question which we intend to pursue, is the ascertainment that there seems to be a discrepancy between what we termed "therapist consciousness" (especially the parts concerning attitudes to alcohol abuse and alcohol related problems) and the therapist's "personal alcohol consumer consciousness". A further analysis of this discrepancy could prove both theoretically important and of great interest for practice.

REFERENCES

Berger, P. & Luckmann, T. (1976). *Den samfundsvidenskabte virkelighed.* København: Lindhardt & Ringhof.

Herskin, B.: *Socialarbejderens arbejdssituation.* København 1980 (The social workers' work situation).

Kvale, S.: Det kvalitative forskningsintervju. i: Broch et al.: *Nyt fra samfundsvidenskaberne.* København, 1979 (The qualitative research interview).

Eneroth, B.: *Grundbok i kvalitativ metod.* Stockholm, 1984 (Reader in qualitative methodology).

Sabroe, K.-E. (1984). *Socialpsykologi.* København: Akademisk forlag. (Social psychology.)

Sabroe, K.-E. (1989). Alcohol Consumer Consciousness. A social psychological perspective on alcohol. Oslo: National Directorate for the Prevention of Alcohol and Drug problems. ICAA, vol. IV, 1-21.

Schutz, A.: *Hverdagslivets sociologi.* København, 1975 (Everyday Sociology).

Willert, S: Tre essays om professionspædagogik for psykologer. *Psykologisk Skriftserie,* Vol. 8, *nr. 2,* Århus 1983 (Three Essays of treatment-pedagogics for psychologists).

9.

ALCOHOL IN SOCIETY.
The Case of Denmark

```
┌─────────────────────────────────────────────────────┐
│                                                     │
│              ALCOHOL IN SOCIETY                     │
│              The Case of Denmark                    │
│                                                     │
└─────────────────────────────────────────────────────┘
```

I Introduction

The presentation in the following draws on an attempt to present information and considerations regarding the situation of alcohol in society from the perspective of a Danish researcher rooted in psychology. Comparing to the original presentation (Sabroe, 1993b), this article is reduced with the sections on frame of understanding and certain data sections. The task was undertaken at the request of the Amsterdam Group, a group established by European alcohol producers, which in collaboration with EU (DG 5) aims at producing a broad scientific analysis of the biomedical, economical, social, cultural role of alcohol in Europe.

In the original presentation of the material it was considered important not only to display empirical findings on alcohol consumption, but also to suggest a frame of understanding of the relation between man (as consumer) and alcohol and to reflect on prevention and research. This frame of understanding has been presented in a greater extent in the articles 1, 3, and 4, meanwhile, and therefore is not to be repeated here. In the three articles the concept of *Alcohol Consumer Consciousness* is introduced and defined as the intervening (psychological) variable, that grasps man's attitudes, meanings, emotions and inclinations of acting towards alcohol. As an extension of this individually based concept an attempt is made to define the mutuality of the (shared) cognitions of the individuals using the concept of *Social Consciousness*. An attempt is also made of defining level of consciousness, suggesting the levels of Active, Adaptive and Passive Alcohol Consumer Consciousness.

The picture of the *actual behaviour* towards alcohol, which appears in section two, has drawn heavily on the Danish research project: "The Danes' Alcohol Consumer Consciousness" (Sabroe, 1989a, Sabroe & Rasmussen, 1994). Most of the presented material has not been published- at the present time - but is expected to be so in the spring of 1994. The data are drawn from surveys carried out in 1988 and 1989 with a representative population of 2000 above the age of 15. The 1989 survey presented the participants with a questionnaire of 100 questions on alcohol, the 1988 survey only included six alcohol questions in a greater survey on crisis behaviour. It is important to stress that data regarding the major variables support a very consistent picture of a Danish alcohol consumption behaviour during at least one-two decades adding new knowledge, however. Changes have taken place in levels of per capita consumption, in ratio of the beverages, in drinking patterns among the social groups etc., but prevailing patterns exist, and maybe represent cultural factors been predominant over a much longer span of years.

In the last two sections considerations on the two topics of alcohol *research* and *prevention* are brought. Regarding *research* it is suggested that an independent European centre of knowledge, information, co-ordination and initiation is established, and six areas in need of extended research are presented. In reflections about *prevention* it is stressed that rational prevention ought to be the ultimate goal, and a systematization of possible central initiated prevention efforts is suggested.

In a very brief form the thinking that has governed the following presentation can be illustrated with figure 1. The elements of the figure have been dealt with in details in articles 1, 3, and 4, but will appear and be discussed in the text briefly.

Fig. 1: Alcohol Consumer Consciousness

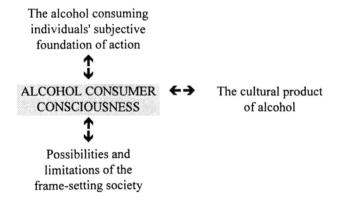

II Alcohol consumption patterns and attitudes

II.1 Alcohol as subject in society

It is obvious that a national population does not present a homogenous picture regarding alcohol consumption patterns regardless of the fact that certain common trends are identifiable. It is so, supposedly, that a greater similarity exists between social groupings (gender, age, social position) across nations belonging to the same region (North-South, beer-wine-spirits areas or alike) than across the same groupings within the nation. But the common trends nevertheless must be expected to be the foundation on which the specific sub-cultural alcohol consumption patterns develop. In the following a Danish alcohol consumption profile will be presented suggesting it could be a prototype for the beer dominated consumption sector of Europe.

Looking for a label to characterize the Danes' relation to alcohol in general one often is offered the concept *liberal* both by experts, politicians and common man. The term is considered to cover conditions that can be described as: relatively *easy availability* of alcohol through retail trade, *few restrictions, little control* but a *fairly high level of excises* and a *readiness* for contribution *from the health and social system* if you become addicted to alcohol. On this background you have a behaviour which in general presents a fairly high level of consumption (by 1991 it is 9.6 l 100% alcohol per capita). In commenting this figure the perspective of abstinence has sometimes been brought forward. Comparing to other countries (especially in a Scandinavian connection) Denmark has a low percentage of total abstinents. In recent investigations the percentage, who stated never having drunk alcohol is 2%. And looking back over the last year only 5% of Danes above the age of 14 have not had alcohol. In Norway and Sweden the figures are four times as big (Hansen & Andersen, 1985). But it is a fact that the consumption is askew distributed in Denmark as in many other countries, dependent on gender, age, income and social group with male, the middle ages (40-50 years) and the higher social groups/incomes as the high consumers. It is also a fact that a minor group of the population (about 16%) consume 50% of the total amount of alcohol.

If one concludes from the two recent major surveys - presented in articles 2 and 3 and in the coming - a picture is obtained which is in accordance with results from investigations in the last decade (Nielsen, 1982; Sælan, 1984; DIKE, 1988; Rasmussen & Sabroe, 1989). The picture - from articles 2 and 3 - supplements with new data, and a few new angles, but the essential message is persistent showing the consistency which is reflected across the variables: sex, age, social group, income, occupation, branch of trade and political party (cf. p. 44 and pp. 65-66). It is mentioned that these variables are not independent of each other, but striking is the unambiguous picture of an increasing consumption of alcohol, nevertheless, when one climbs up the social status ladder, an increasing consumption when you are placed in the advantageous positions on the labour market and an increasing consumption when earnings are high. It is the men from these positions, middle in life, who proportionally have the highest consumption of alcohol, and for these men the consumption of wine plays a comparatively great role, as it does for the women of the same age from these groups, beer being the predominant type of alcohol, however. And all in all, one can conclude that it seems as if high consumption of alcohol does not represent a poverty-culture as has so often been presented in the stereotypes, being present in the population and supported by the public media. Rather, it is a sign of belongingness to a culture of affluence, of having a surplus economically and socially. Considerations along the line of life-style differences is just around the corner presented with such assumptions. But we have to put up a warning. The results do not present individual characteristics, it is cultural and group patterns we are dealing with, no one is judged by his or her belonging to any of the presented groupings. When characterizing the situation one often (from health authorities, experts, politicians) states that 90% of all alcohol consumers in Denmark enjoy alcohol without problems. Two to four percent are considered to have a serious addiction problem damaging for health and social life, while 6-8% are regarded as heavy consumers with alcohol related problems to a lesser or greater degree, for the major part being able to maintain a working-life, however.

The reason, that the label liberal is so readily produced, maybe also is - besides the descriptive value of the term as such - that, being a member of the Scandinavian community comparison is often undertaken with the other Scandinavian countries (Finland, Norway, Iceland and Sweden). Compared with the restrictive alcohol policy in these countries (with regard to availability, control and price), Denmark can truly be characterized as liberal. It should be pointed out that liberal is purely a descriptive term and not employed as a value concept, as used in this connection.

If we go five-ten years back placing the term liberal in connection with alcohol policy at a positive position on a value scale undoubtedly would have had an extensive support. Supposedly, it is still so that a majority will accept this atti-

tude. But changes have appeared in the later years suggesting for example an ex-
panded control with public drinking, a lower BAC-level regarding driving, prohibition of alcohol at work places etc., and support to suggestions alike appears
to be growing. These changes to a higher degree seem to be based on value and
attitude changes in the population than on alcohol policy oriented initiatives
from the government. The governments and the "Folketing" (Danish Parliament)
has acted through the last four-five years with regard to alcohol related problems, however, but in a way considered incoherent by many. On the one hand,
the Government/"Folketing" closed down the (independent) *Alcohol and Narcotics Council* under the Ministry of Health and transferred the civil servants from
the Council to offices in the Health Department, in 1990. It also discontinued the
special function of *Alcohol and Narcotics Consultant to the Ministry of Education*, in 1991. But on the other hand a "Government Board on Prevention" has
been established and with reference to that another advisory group called
"Alcohol Policy Forum". Members of both these boards represent central authorities and private organisations oriented towards alcohol prevention and treatment
and also include representatives from the temperance movement. The results of
these new government initiatives are not obvious at present, the Board and the
Forum having been working for just over three years. In the autumn of 1993,
further developments took place. A law of actions towards alcohol abuse was
passed, among other things giving means to research and intervention and
establishing a parliamentary committee to deal with the distribution of the means
and setting priorities.

A central thinking behind the alcohol policy outlined above is that alcohol behaviour ought to be the result of the individuals free and responsible (conscious)
acting with regard to alcohol (see also p. 15ff). The responsibility perspective is
found in the legislative principle "that sober man carries the responsibility for
drunken man's deed", also. In general no excuse is accepted in Danish Courts of
having been drunk, when committing crime. Central dictated restrictions have
been regarded as counter-productive in relation to the efforts of de-dramatizing
the connection alcohol and man, a set goal for the alcohol policy of governments
for the last three-four decades. Prevention, as it previously has been, still today is
the central alcohol policy theme, therefore. But an increase seems to take place
with regard to general and specific campaigns, issuing information, suggesting
rules, giving norms (of "healthy drinking") etc. Altogether, the descriptive term
of liberal still seems best to cover the Danish situation regarding alcohol, however.

Some recent results from a representative Danish survey support this statement (Sabroe, 1990). Asking people (in an open question) to give reasons for drinking respective not drinking alcohol, we find the *reasons to drink* alcohol connected with *positive aspects of life*, only a very little minority stating problem oriented reasons. *Reasons not to drink* are mainly attributed to *driving* and *negative health risks*. Only few give statements connected with abuse, dependence etc. (cf. article 6, tables 1 and 2).

People do recognize the potential risks of consuming alcohol, 76% of the population states that alcohol is a potential risk factor, while only one out of four is of the opinion that alcohol could be positive for health. But 76% of the population also states that alcohol is a good in their lives generally (table 1). It also seems as if the population in general recognizes the effect of alcohol and rather precisely knows how much to drink without being intoxicated (more about that p. 165).

Table 1   Opinions on alcohol as good or risk

---

a. Alcohol has a positive influence on health

Yes	24.2%
No	68.1%
Do not know	7.5%
No answer	0.1%

b. Alcohol has a negative influence on health

Yes	76.0%
No	17.5%
Do not know	6.4%
No answer	0.1%

c. Alcohol as good or bad in life

Generally a good	76.3%
Generally a bad	9.4%
Don't know	14.0%
No answer	0.3%

It is evident that an alcohol consumer consciousness, of which the substance alcohol enters into positive connections (in its cognitive anchoring and emotional constraint) is a historical product. The alcohol consumer consciousness is not fixed or unalterable. It is the result of the individuals' mutual relations with the surroundings, in which the economical, legal, general and specific cultural frames are important for its development. The individual alcohol-user behaviour, resulting herefrom, also will be "historically determined" carrying along the socially set conditions, therefore, but in its concrete amplification representing the individual's elaboration of these conditions.

If we look behind the average figures of experiencing alcohol as a good, but also as a health risk, we find the greatest support for the opinion of alcohol as a good in the age groups of 20-50 years with 80%, and among the higher social groups, higher educated and higher incomes 85% support that alcohol is a good in life (table 2). For the health risk we find that a little more women than men choose to give this answer. When asked why a negative influence, the most frequent answer was (two out of five) that a "heavy consumption was a health risk" (table 3). Men are more heavily represented among the almost 25%, who find that alcohol benefits the health. When the respondents were asked to qualify the answer of benefit for health, more than half added "healthy in small quantities" and often named 1-3 drinks a day. Interesting is that among these 25% one finds more elderly than young. In the age group above 50 years 35% gives support to the opinion, while only 8% below the age of 20 supports that alcohol is good for health (table 4).

Table 2. Considering alcohol as a good in life

Population in general	76%
Age group of 20-50 years	80%
Highest social groups	85%
Higher income groups	85%
Higher education groups	85%

Table 3. Considering alcohol a health risk

Population in general	76%
Men	71%
Women	80%

Table 4. Considering alcohol a benefit for health

Population in general	24.2%
Men	28.6%
Women	20.1%
Age < 20 years	8.0%
Age > 50 years	35.0%

The stressing in the "alcohol policy" of the individuals' responsibility for his or her own life and of an alcohol behaviour, founded on knowledge and information, is mirrored in the general behaviour of the population. At least until recently, it has been a common attitude that a man's (woman's) drinking was his/her own responsibility and one did not interfere in relation to seemingly heavy consumption, unless one belonged to the closest of relatives (spouse or alike). The opinion that (the level of) alcohol consumption is a personal matter has been under attack from health authorities in their general prevention campaigns but also in the *work life* specifically. Joint efforts have been undertaken from employers' and employees' organizations in establishing alcohol policies at enterprise level, regulating the consumption of alcohol in the workplace (a *preventive* effort) and giving opportunity for support should one has developed alcohol-related problems (*counselling* and *treatment*) (Grunnet & Bang, 1991; Sabroe, 1992d).

It has been claimed in the debate on prevention that the knowledge of health related risk of heavy drinking is poor, maybe except the relationship with liver cirrhosis. But the results presented above indicate, that at least an acknowledged general relationship exists in the population between alcohol and health. Irrespective of that this acknowledged relation apparently (together with other risk factors) is an element of consciousness, a positive world of experience around alcohol is present in the population, however, illustrated in the responses to the question on reasons to drink alcohol.

One could postulate that there is a contradiction in this picture. On the one hand responses to survey questions etc. always should be evaluated in relation to the situation they are thought belonging to, and "health" and "daily life" are not necessarily "merging concepts". But, on the other hand, in matter of explanation it could also be argued that the two convictions of health risk and life-good exist "side by side" in the consciousness, and an intervening variable, which with Schiøler (1987) could be named "*cultural immunity*", incurs and constitutes the individual behavior, causing that the acknowledged risk of health "is not subjectively experienced as real". Alcohol becomes a *consumer-goods*, which is used with thoughtfulness and unproblematic by the vast majority of the population. An appropriate daily consumption "eliminates" for the overall majority the (acknowledged) health risk connected with alcohol, and the experienced positive effects (especially as social "lubricant" and means of relish) obtain priority and can be expressed in the statement that alcohol in general is a good in life. Attention should be brought to the documented fact, however, that people often possess an individual experience of immunity with regard to alcohol risks. It is reflected through data showing, that when asked about the *risk* alcohol carries for the single individual, it is placed relatively low on an impact scale, in comparison with other subjects considered having risk potentialities. *But* when asked the same question about alcohol as a risk in general for the population, it is placed in the high end compared with other subjects (Hansen et al., 1991; Sjøberg, 1991). Alcohol is the subject showing the greatest difference in position in the two risk-scales, among twenty subjects.

If the goal of prevention is a reduction, this raises a problem. How does one communicate in reduction terms about a matter, which is not experienced as hostile in relation to the individuals' own situation? It is my opinion that a choice of arguments with *insight character* (extended consciousness) and *not submissive character* (passive resignation) is important. In the terms of the understanding presented in article 1, the aim must be to establish an *active Alcohol Consumer Consciousness*. (For further considerations around prevention see p. 173ff).

II.2 Specific alcohol behaviours

It is obvious from public data, that a change in consumption patterns has taken place during the last four-five decades among the Danes. It is true as well with regard to the amount consumed as with the relative distribution across the different types of alcohol, and the situations in which it is consumed (table 5). The picture of a rise across the entire period is not true, however. In fact a peak was reached in 1983 and a decline of about 13% has taken place in the succeeding period.

Table 5 Alcohol consumption 1960-1990

Litre 100% ethanol per capita:	1960	1970	1980	1990
	4.4	7.0	9.4	9.6
Beer	74%	70%	64%	61%
Wine	9%	10%	20%	25%
Spirits	17%	20%	16%	14%

The change applies to the alcohol consumation at different social strata, over age and between the sexes, also. Some trends seem to be that the age of alcohol debut has become lower, that a rise in amount of consumption has taken place among the young age groups, that women relatively to men have raised their share of the total consumption, that women and men in the higher social groups and educations are approaching an equal consumption (Nielsen, 1982; Hansen & Andersen, 1985; Sabroe 1989 & 1991) (See also p. 159). Denmark still is pre-dominantly a "beer nation", but the share of wine of the total consumption has nearly tripled over the three decades from 1960-1990, while the beer and spirits shares have been reduced with about 18% both.

Further trends are related to a movement towards consumption with meals. In modern times alcohol has never been considered a nutriment within the Danish culture. But it does not mean that alcohol and food are unrelated. On the con-trary, today consuming alcohol to a fairly high degree takes place in relation to lunch and evening meals. "Frokostbajer" (lunch-beer) has for years been a con-cept in Danish culture with positive connotations, and it still is. A development has occurred, however, having the result that - at least during the work week - drinking "Frokostbajer" does not happen so often. But the major connection between alcohol and food is mirrored in the rather great change in the percent-ages covered by the single types of alcohol. The growth in the wine consumption is connected with the fact, that consumption of alcohol with evening meals and especially with the week-end meals has nearly become a tradition, and wine to a greater degree than beer is a food-companion. In a recent investigation this has been proved by extensive data from a representative population of 2000 Danes (Sabroe & Rasmussen, 1994).

Taken into account the total amount of consumers one finds a peak at 18 hours and in all more than half of the consumption in a day takes place in the five hours between 18 and 23 in the evening. A small peak also shows up around lunch time (fig. 3). Breaking the figures down in relation to gender (fig. 4), one finds the well-known difference in level, but the distributions of men and women, respectively, are very similar, indicating a to a high degree shared consumption situation.

Figure 2: Alcohol consumption (in total)
over 24 hours

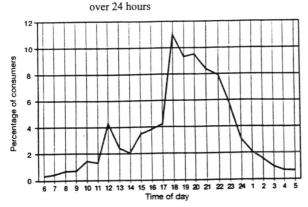

Figure 3: Alcohol consumption (gender)
over 24 hours

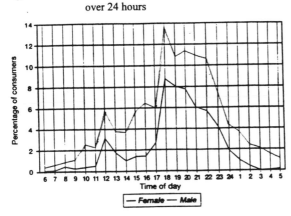

Looking over a period of 15-20 years it seems as if a change has taken place in which alcohol consumption has moved from work life and public drinking to drinking in the evenings (at home) and especially in the week-ends (also at home) (Hansen & Andersen, 1985; Socialstyrelsen, 1991; Sabroe, 1989 & 1991). But habits (acquired from other cultures?) have established patterns of alcohol consumation outside meals, in the way that a time-out drink has been common between coming home from work and the evening meal, for example. But our research also indicates that an after-meal drink seems to come up (Sabroe & Rasmussen, 1994). Further our research and other sources (Colling, 1989) indicate that though the movement from work life consumption to home life consumption has taken place, there are places in which the "Fyraftensbajer" (knock-off timebeer) is kept in tradition. Another (newer) tradition of outside-the-meal drinking is of more national origin, being the "Bitter" (Herb-alcohol, spirit concentration) which is "used" to start a social encounter (in private life) especially in the morning, or as a starter in connection with negotiations (in commercial or organizational life). "The Bitter" also has been connected to outdoor recreational activities, to a high degree.

In general alcohol consumption is a social affair in Denmark, and most frequent it takes place within the family. This dominating trend seems to have been persistent for many years and runs across the different socio-biographical groupings of society. If a difference could be found it might be in relation to social strata. Men from the lower social group are displaying a difference to women in the amount consumed which could indicate that relatively more alcohol for men from these groups is consumed outside the family (table 15). In Sabroe & Rasmussen (1994), specific data will be brought regarding the situation and place in which alcohol is consumed.

Table 6 Alcohol consumption ratio according to social group

	High	Social Group				Low
		1	2	3	4	5
Male		1.3	1.6	1.8	2.2	3.3
Female		1	1	1	1	1

When considering the types of alcohol: beer, wine and spirits, we obtain the distributions shown in fig. 4. It is obvious that spirits consumption is quite different from the other two beverages with a fairly low level throughout the day and only displaying a minor raise in the later night hours. There is a certain similarity regarding the distributions of beer and wine, the difference being that beer is the dominating beverage during the forenoon and afternoon, while following the same trend as wine from dinner time and throughout the night.

Fig. 4: Consumption (types of alcohol)

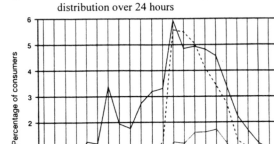

distribution over 24 hours

In general the Danes' alcohol consumption takes place at home. Different investigations give figures from about 55 to 65% (Sundhedsstyrelsen, 1991; Sabroe & Rasmussen, 1994), and if you add what could be termed "homely settings like with family or friends the figures raise to 75-80%. On this background it can be of no surprise that the most frequent drinking companion is a spouse or concubinary (about 60%), and family and friends are counting for 30%. The amount drinking alone are in Sabroe & Rasmussen (1994) calculated to just over 5%.

As previously indicated it also appears that alcohol today is consumed to a great extent accompanying a meal or adjacent to a meal as pre and after meal drinks. It seems as if alcohol (that is beer and wine) through the later years have been much more common as the liquid-accompaniment of meals. This (new) consumption again seems to be additional to a traditional pattern and could be regarded as part of the cause behind the rise in the per capita consumption from the 50's to the 80's. Maintaining the fairly high level and looking at the consumption patterns one could argue that the tradition of having alcohol with your meal has obtained a footing in a greater part of the population.

One aspect which might be derived from this is, that consumption of alcohol purely with the purpose of effect (intoxication) is not predominant. If one takes the relatively small figures representing consumption at restaurants, bars etc. one finds that 63% only drink with meals, while 21% seldom or never have food while drinking in public. The non-intoxication oriented drinking behaviour is supported by results also indicating that 70% of the population has to go back more than one month to remember the last time they experienced being intoxicated (also including slightly under the influence), 46% even state that they have to go more than a year back (Rasmussen & Sabroe, 1989; Sabroe & Rasmussen, 1994).

The data used in the tables above is based on the percentage of consumers displaying the behaviour. The data in fig. 5 are derived from the amount consumed and proves that more are consumed when taking wine, the average being one and a half unit per hour compared to beer with one unit per hour (fig. 6).

Figure 5: Average amount consumed
over 24 hours

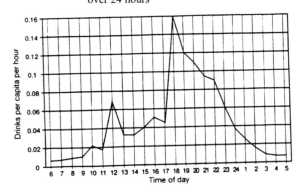

Figure 6: Consumption density
over 24 hours

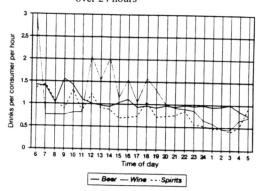

When age is brought in, we get a picture which disclose quite different patterns. In fig. 7 is shown the distribution of consumed drinks per capita per hour throughout a day. As can be seen the elderly, but also the middle ages have the characteristic peaks around lunch and dinner, while the younger age groups (<30 years) do not have a lunch peak and the maximum consumption is two hours later than for the two other age groups. At present data is not available, that can be used explanatory to this, but some further details will appear in Sabroe & Rasmussen (1994). Possible reasons for the different distribution in the young age group could be that they generally eat later or that the meal is a "fast" one, and alcohol consumption is postponed to a later leisure period. Another line of reasoning could be that the young in the later years establish themselves in families later than preceeding generations, and that consumption of alcohol is with friends, meaning an evening activity. Also the question - for those being in a core-family situation - of haivng small children could be a factor worthwhile considering.

Fig. 7A: Alcohol consumption
according to age

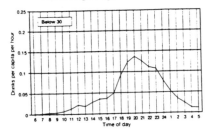

Fig. 7B: Alcohol consumption
according to age

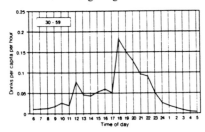

Fig. 7C: Alcohol Consumption
according to age

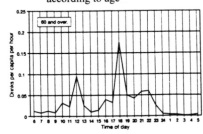

The data being the foundation of most of the considerations above have been the reported consumption of alcohol over the last 24 hours. Results have also been obtained regarding the consumption for each day a week back. In figure 8 the distribution of the week is shown. It proved that the week-days have almost identical patterns, while the week-end has to be split into Friday-Saturday and Sunday. The dominant week-end consumption is clearly demonstrated. Figure 9 brings evidence to the fact, that similar patterns exist regarding the three types of alcohol although the rise in amount of consumers in the weekend is more marked for wine. Being presented with relatively firm patterns, it is worthwhile to draw in the result, however, that asked if they have any regular alcohol-use habits only one out of six says yes. 80% of the population state that they have no regular alcohol-consumption habits. It has been discussed in the project group if the answers to the question represent an interpretation of the word habit in which the "bad" connotations have been predominant. It is often so that when you in Danish talk about "habits" the association "bad habits" is very ready. This might in particular be true when the subject is a "touchy" one as alcohol.

Fig. 8: Consumption (in total)
according to day of week

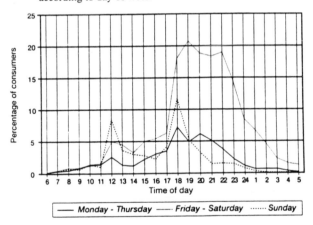

Fig. 9: Consumption (type of alcohol)
distribution over the week

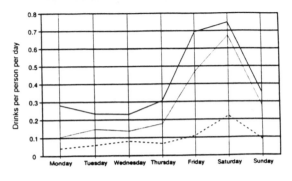

It appears that the individual has a rather realistic experience of what amount of alcohol brings him/her into a state "of feeling under the influence of alcohol", *men* on the average report *five drinks* (drink: equal to 12 gr. of alcohol) and *women three drinks*. If taken within a shorter time period (e.g. two hours) this amount will bring the BAC level on the average ("normal" weight person) to about 1 per thousand, a figure that for example exceeds the level accepted for car-driving (BAC level of 0.8 per thousand).

When looking at the situations in which the population have stated being intoxicated last time, it displays a distribution which indicates that "normally" it takes place in the daily-life surroundings (table 7). But the dominance of family and close friends (and not solely the spouse) also indicates that intoxication presumably often takes place at special occasions.

Table 7. Companion with whom last intoxicated

Last intoxicated with	
Spouse (alone)	30%
Family	20%
Close friends	26%
Colleagues	13%
Alone	10%
Others	1%

It was previously mentioned that the Danes at the one hand considered alcohol in general to be a good in their life, and on the other hand acknowledged the potential risks connected with alcohol consumption. If you ask about health *consequences of alcohol consumption*, 65% of the population is of the opinion that drinking below four units a day your health-risk is negligible, 10% find that you can drink up to ten units. The remainder is divided between undecided (15%), and that it is a person-dependent relationship (10%).

II.3. Alcohol in traditions and rituals

It is sometimes said mockingly that a Dane has not only the right to drink alcohol whenever and in which situations he wants, but that he has almost an obligation to do it. This of course is an extreme pointing out the claimed liberal attitude to alcohol consumption in Denmark. But in a great majority of social rites - among others christening, confirmation, wedding, anniversaries, adult birthdays, jubilees, achievement celebrations, inaugurations - alcohol plays a role, in many ways used to characterize the situation as special. In later years, it has become an everyday custom, also, that you offer a beer or a glass of other types of alcohol alongside or replacing coffee or tea, receiving guests for shorter or informal visits. Though uniform patterns exist for social rites across the social groupings, there is subcultural differences in relation to which type of beverages is served and in which amount. In general intoxication will not be desired, but it is not infrequent as a consequence especially at certain of the social rites (e.g. confirmation).

The confirmation (normally at the age of 14) in many families will be the occasion at which the youngster for the first time *officially* drink alcohol, also. In table 8 a distribution is shown of a representative population's own statements of alcohol debut age, and in table 9 are shown the results, from the same population, of a question asking when children/youngsters should be allowed to drink alcohol without an adult present. The attitudes seem to be a little more restrictive than what actually takes place.

Table 8. Age having alcohol debut

Age	Percentage
9-10	4%
11	1%
12	6%
13	8%
14	16%
15	14%
16	10%
17	8%
18	7%
Under 9 or over 18	1%
Unanswered	10%

Table 9. Age suggested for alcohol debut

When should children be allowed to drink alcohol
with adults being present?

Age	Percentage
< 13	0.5%
13	1%
14	7%
15	17%
16	20%
17	9%
18	27%
> 18	1%
Unanswered	16.5%

II 4. Alcohol in problem oriented connection

As previously stated, central or public control of alcohol consumption through an extensive and restrictive alcohol policy has not been the custom in Denmark. The individual and his or her closest relations have been the agents of actions related to consequences of abuse. It is obvious that the Danish alcohol policy sets out from the opinion that the individual consumer carries the responsibility for an abuse of alcohol. Taking to excessive drinking is a "choice", and remedy of the situation must be found with the individual. But it is obvious also, that society must have and do accept a responsibility for certain regulations offering alcohol as a legal way of obtaining an altered state of consciousness (intoxicated), and must be ready with support, treatment or alike, should the individual - "given" this "offer and choice" - get alcohol related problems.

In the Danish society alcohol is considered to play a role in creating social problems for families and breaking careers. The most recent figures from the Ministry of Health (Sundhedsstyrelsen, 1991) asserts that 250,000 Danes (of an adult population of about 4,000,000) can be considered heavy consumers of alcohol, meaning that they drink considerably more than the recommended (relatively risc-free) 21 units (male) or 14 units (female) per week. Figures concerning family consequences are difficult to establish and no official registration exists. A few available results are that 100 children out of approx. 46,000 births per year have signs of fetal alcohol syndrome and that about 8,000 out of 15,000 children placed outside their families by authorities are in one way or other connected with alcohol-related problems in the families. Details are available for alcohol related diseases, and seen in total the figures calculated for *alcohol related death* are for the last half of the 80's showing a relatively constant picture (table 10). The consumption over the period has been slightly declining (12-13%) having decreased from a peak in 1983.

Table 10. Death from an alcohol-related disease pr. 100.000 inhabitants above the age of 14.

	1985	1986	1987	1988	1989
Death pr. 100.000	22.3	22.6	22.5	22.6	25.2

In *juridical connection* alcohol does not seem to create any major problem with regard to smuggling and clandestine destillation. But police statistics and figures from the Criminology Research Group (Kramp, 1990) states that in 1988 50% of the persons arrested were under the influence of alcohol, that 25% of the imprisoned previously have been under alcohol treatment, that 12% are under alcohol treatment when committing the act, and that 16% of the imprisoned find themselves that they are in need for alcohol treatment.

Regarding *alcohol and traffic* data shows that alcohol related traffic accidents with person damage have declined 18% through the last five years, and in 1989 amounts to 19.9% of all person-damage traffic accidents (a stable figure through the last five years). When considering alcohol related traffic deaths, the percentage is 29.8 of all traffic deaths, which is a decline of 4% in a five year period. Recent figures from police statistics seems to indicate that the decline in alcohol related traffic incidents in particular takes place among the younger age groups (Politiets Årsberetninger, 1992).

The relation between alcohol abuse and crime seems to be present, but it is not easy to define. Supposedly there is no direct causal relationship, but alcohol could be part of a tainted social background of the offender and abuse maybe more existing as an intervening variable.

In Sabroe (1992) a *group-oriented profile of the heavy consumer* has been established. When drawing on the results from (ibid.) we find:

1) Heavy consumers of alcohol are found six times more frequent among men than among women

2) In average, heavily consuming women are younger than heavily consuming men. (Women most frequent in their 30's, men in the 40-50 years of age).

3) Relatively seen, the upper social groups have more heavy consumers of alcohol. In these groups the ratio of men-women is approximately 3 to 1 (about the same as the ratio for normal consumption), whereas the ratio in the lowest social group regarding heavy consumption is 9 (men) to 1 (women).

4) Relatively seen, the high income groups have most heavy consumers across gender and social group.

5) Heavy consumers are relatively more frequent found in the highest placed group at the labour market.

6) Regarding branches of trade the building and construction sector has twice as many heavy consumers as should be expected, while the social and health sector has eight times fewer.

III Alcohol research

A major problem in research on alcohol culture and alcohol consumption patterns is the lack of longitudinal research. If you are looking for genuine indicators of how alcohol consumption changes over periods of individual life, and through historical periods, it is a necessity to have access to data, that follow the individual in his/her development in a changing society. But it is also evident that such data - obviously being of a restricted dimension - need to be mirrored in greater samples of representative data acquired through cross sectional analysis. One question which producer, retailer, health authorities, governments would like to have answered all is, if there are common denominators counting for the alterations of patterns which we see through periods of time, and why seemingly there is a great inertia regarding people's alcohol consumer behaviour. The question has been raised if personal income, taxation, price policy, availability, individual taste, group pressure, life-cycle etc. plays a role, and quite a bit of research has been carried out trying to establish a connection between one or more of these or other variables and consumption. Some have claimed to have established the causal relationship, but few have survived in a scrutinous rechecking. Some as price and availability are brought forward again and again, however.

Alcohol research is undertaken in varying degree throughover Europe, both governmentally and privately funded. The differences are great and unfortunately Denmark has been placed very low on the investment scale until recently regarding funding for alcohol research. But the situation is positively changing, and major steps forward might be obtained, if "the pressure" through a common European co-ordination and initation of research is established. An organization to that purpose *could* be established within the EU, but *maybe* an *independent* organization would be a better choice supported by governments and alcohol industries . The aims should be at least fourfold and comprise:

1) Acting as a *Centre of Knowledge* to be at the disposal of authorities in Europe with information.

2) Acting as an *Information Centre* to be of assistance to researchers in Europe.

3) Acting as *Co-ordination Centre* for researchers in Europe.

4) Acting as a *Initiation Centre* for research in Europe.

The centre ought to have a cross scientific staff of qualified researchers (besides administration). The researchers should act according to the four aims but not necessarily do research themselves, although this would be preferable.

When looking at point 4 above, some of the research area pressing to be undertaken are:

1) *Children and alcohol*: How and when does alcohol become established in the mind of children, and how is the development of attitudes towards alcohol throughout the childhood and adolescence? Are fundamental relations established, determinative for adult consumption? Are national or international trends identifiable regarding the question of children's view of/ relation with alcohol?

2) *Adolescence, youngsters and alcohol*: Throughout Europe changes in relation to traditional drinking patterns seem to take place. What is the initiator of these changes? Are similar patterns present across nations? Which are the consequences of these changes regarding behaviour of the young people? Do families or societies react on the changes in consumption patterns?

3) *Alcohol policy and national drinking patterns*: A relatively great amount of research has been dealing with effects of alcohol policy efforts. A certain consistency is claimed by many regarding effects of the price instrument and availability, but others dispute this. There is a need to have a major international investigation, that takes in the entire "alcohol picture" and not only look at official total consumption figures. How is the distribution across the population under specific alcohol policy conditions? What about illegal production and border trade; rise or fall in alcohol related criminality, health indicators, traffic casualties, illegal drugs etc.?

4) *Alcohol and health*: Assuming that a majority regard alcohol as a good in their life, but at the same time acknowledge the risks, it will be important to pursue a research that is directed towards the possible beneficial effects opposite the risks in consuming alcohol. One reason for the importance of this area is of course the dispute about alcohol (in moderate quantity) as a health precaution.

5) *Alcohol related problems*: One major research problem is to establish a primary prevention, and as part of that trying to establish early indicators of a possible route towards alcohol abuse. International co-operation would be of greatest importance in this delicate research area. Another research problem under this heading is to establish models for calculating the expenditure of society in dealing with alcohol misuse. Cost figures will be part of any debate dealing with alcohol policy, but are often given so vastly different by various authorities that they have a tendency to ruin the debate.

6) *Alcohol abuse and therapy*: Investigations of treatment outcome are very difficult to carry out and often demand a prolonged research process - stretching over years - if done properly. The results vary immensely in their indication of therapy outcome, a good deal even being rather pessimistic. It would be important to have an international study following some of the major therapeutic orientations (in general), but trying also to establish, if a possible connection could be found between specific therapies and types of misuse/misuser.

As stated above it is an adamant demand that an international office/organization co-ordinating alcohol research in Europe is cross-scientific manned. But is also important to ensure that scientific methodology is represented in its variety, meaning broadly stated that as well quantitative as qualitative oriented research should be represented.

IV Prevention of alcohol misuse

As a basic assumption we shall postulate that no rational prevention of alcohol related problems can be established without a profound knowledge of, how alcohol exists as a subject in the population's daily life, and a knowledge of the function alcohol fulfils in a cultural perspective. Central to the understanding is the alcohol consumer consciousness of the population, and the ultimate goal in any society having alcohol as a consumer goods must be to create the conditions for an *active alcohol consumer consciousness*. As the individuals' foundation for acting in relation to alcohol the consumer consciousness is embedded in the complicated pattern including the consuming individual with his/her subjective foundation of acting, the society setting the possibilities and limitations for the consumption and the existence of the cultural product of alcohol. Central is also the supplementary conviction that the wish of health and quality of life is deeply embedded in the individual and that (being sane) we do not purposedly do damage to ourselves.

Prevention is often closely related to an alcohol policy, and creating an alcohol policy is a delicate matter. You do not create an alcohol policy at random, it must be founded in the history and culture of a country, it must take into account the prevailing alcohol consumption patterns and it must be consistent with the population's alcohol consumer consciousness. An alcohol policy is neither given once and for all. It is a product of a dynamic interplay of many different and changing interests and has to be actively kept up, but also permanently developed.

The aim of prevention: health is a multifaceted concept, the delimitation/definition of which must draw on a multiplicity of sciences with medicine, psychology and sociology being central. But health is difficult to define because it is a qualitative concept and a compiling concept for a broad fan of relations, which enters into antagonistic connections, of which the opposite pole is illness of somatic, psychic or social origin. It is with such a frame that alcohol related problems must be considered, and the offers of causal relations, which everybody of course is anxious to find, are many. They reach from disease pathogenesis to convictions, which look at heavy consumption (with its risk of alcohol related problems) as a life-style consequence, as the result of concrete circumstances of life, as the result of (social) environment conditions etc.

Both in prevention and in establishing an alcohol policy it is decisive whether you choose use or misuse as the basis. A rational prevention must take use of alcohol as point of origin, not forgetting the *misuse* as a possible outcome. Trying to systematize the agents of prevention regarding the alcohol area, a picture could be like fig. 11.

Fig. 11. Agents of alcohol misuse prevention

---

1. Legal control

- Legislation of licensed premises
- Number of placed allowed to sell alcohol
- Opening hours
- Limitation of sale by retail
- Number of types of alcohol allowed
- Age criteria for purchasing alcohol
- Rationing in general
- Alcohol prohibition in certain social surroundings
- Prohibition for certain types of alcohol
- Limitations of production in general or for specific types of alcohol
- Traffic legislation (BAC level)
- Prohibition of private alcohol production
- Crime legislation (drunken behaviour etc.)
- Prohibition of advertising
- Alcohol free geographical areas

2. Price policy

- Excise of alcohol in general
- Special tax for public serving of alcohol

3. General education and public information

- Factual knowledge about alcohol
- Attitude influence directed towards appropriate alcohol behaviour
- Attitude influence directed towards abstinence

4. Counselling of concrete person/groups in potential danger

5. Treatment of persons with alcohol related problems.

The list covers as well primary as secondary and tertiary prevention. If we compare international experiences of these means of prevention, it is obvious that results are ambiguous. Same type of means have produced diverse results and longitudinal effects do not seem to be prominent.

When considering prevention from a governmental perspective a matrix as shown in fig. 12 could be descriptive of the approaches:

Fig. 12. Central initiated prevention efforts

		FOUNDATION OF PREVENTION				
	IDEA OF PREVENTION	INTERVEN-TION PERSPECTIVE	MAJOR ORIEN-TATION IN THE PREVENTION	EXPERIENCED USER-ALCO-HOL RELATION	UNDERLYING SENTIMENT	ORIENTATION
P R E V E N T I O N	1. Life risk control	Restrictions	Prohibition legislation	Abuse	Guilt, fear, anxiety	CLOSED MIND
	2. Life risk prevention	Protection	Warning information			
E F F O R T S	3. Life quality maintenance	Guidance	Special educa-tion with councelling perspective	Use	Trust, Understanding	OPEN MIND
	4. Life quality development	Responsibility	Extended education with action per-spective			

Effort *one* is a closed and restriction oriented approach, *two* is closed in orientation but also information oriented. In *three* openness and a systematic educational orientation is dominant, and *four* combine openness with a knowledge and informal socialization oriented approach. The matrix of course only illustrates "ideal forms" using the criteria of idea, perspective, sentiment and orientation, and in practice the picture will be a mingling. But in relation to the individual acting towards alcohol, one could imagine that approach 1 and 2 to a high degree were related with an adaptive consumer consciousness, and 3 and 4 with an active consumer consciousness as defined page 20-21.

When considering preventive efforts from a governmental perspective three major questions ought to be answered:

1. How does the population (various subgroups) experience alcohol as subject in society, and how is alcohol related problems "placed" (individual/social of origin)?

2. Which are the expectations of the population regarding the public's attitude to alcohol related problems?

3. What does the population consider as alcohol related problems at all? How is "the responsibility" for the existence of alcohol related problems placed?

It is questions of which scattered and sporadic knowledge exists, but research is strongly needed.

Supposedly a thorough understanding of the existence of alcohol related problems in a society - and by that the foundation for an alcohol policy and prevention - cannot be obtained without a wholeness thinking, which departs from the present situation, but also look ahead. The identification of which factors comprises a wholeness perspective is an important research task.

Notes

1   This division of the concept is in debt to the crisis research at the Institute of Psychology (Petersen, E., Sabroe, K.-E., Kristensen, O.S., Sommerlund, B. (1987). Danskernes tilværelse under krisen I-II. Aarhus: Aarhus Universitetsforlag. ('Danes during the Crisis'). There is also a certain relation to Hilgard's presentation (Hilgard, E. (1980) Consciousness. Annual Review Psychology, vol. 31, 1-13.)

2   The parties are represented in the Danish Parliament at the moment (1992) with the following amount of seats: Social Democrats: 55, Conservative: 35, Socialist People's Party 24, The Left Party 22, Progress Party: 16, The Radical Left 10, Centrum Democrats: 9, The Christian People's Party: 4.

References

Calahan, D. (1987) *Understanding America's drinking problem*. San Fransisco, Jossey-Bass.

Colling, H. (1989) *Alkohol og arbejdsliv*. København: Socialforskningsinstituttet. Rap. 89-16.

Danielson, A. (1982). Tegningsanalyse af seksårige børns tegninger af mennesker, der drikker alkohol. In: I. Nelson-Löfgren, Bo Löfgren & A. Danielson: *Barns Förestāllninger om Alkohol*. Stockholm: Socialstyrelsen.

Durkheim, E. (1972) *Den sociologiske metode*. København: Gyldendal (opr. 1985).

Edwards, G. (1982) *The treatment of drinking problems*. London: Grant, McIntyre.

Edwards, G. et al. (1977) *Alcohol related disabilities*. Geneva: World Health Organization.

Elmeland, K., Nygaard, P., & Sabroe, K.-E. (1990) Storbrugere. 12 fortællinger om alkohol. *Psykologisk Skriftserie, 15, no. 1.*

Everett, C.; Wadell, B. & Heath, D.B. (Eds.) (1976) *Cross cultural approaches to the study of alcohol*, New York: Morton Publishers.

Grunnet, K. & Bang, H.J. (1991) *Alkoholpolitik og medarbejderudvikling*. København: Dansk Arbejdsgiverforening.

Hansen, E.J. & Andersen, D. (1985) *Alkoholforbrug og alkoholpolitik*. København: SFI, publik. 145.

Hansen, W.B., Raynor, A.E., Wolkenstein, B.H. (1991) Perceived personal immunity to the consequences of drinking alcohol. *Journal of Behavioral Medicine, 14*, 205-224.

Kramp, P. (1990). *Alkoholvaner blandt kriminalforsorgens klientel*. København: Justitsministeriet. (Alcohol habits among criminals)

Ledermann, S. (1956) *Alcool, Alcoolisme, alcoolisation. Données scientifique de caractère physiologue, economique et social*. Paris: Presse Universitaires de France.

Lemmens, P. (1991) *Measurements and distributions of alcohol consumption*. Den Haag: CIP-Gegevens Koninklijke Bibliotheek.

Marshall, M. (Ed.) (1979) *Beliefs, behavior and alcohol beverages*. Ann Arbor: Michigan Univ. Press.

McCarthy, D., Morrison, S. & Mills. K.C. (1983) Attitudes, Beliefs and Alcohol Use. *Journals of Studies on Alcohol, 44*, No. 2, 328-341.

Mäkelä, K. (1986) Attitudes towards drinking and drunkenness in four Scandinavian countries. In Babor, T. (Ed.) *Alcohol and Culture*. New York: Annuals of the N.Y. Academy of Sciences, vol. 472.

Nielsen, K. (1982) *Danskernes alkoholvaner*. København: Alkohol- og Narkotikarådet.

Petersen, E., Sabroe, K.-E., & Kristensen, O.S. (1987) *Danskernes tilværelse under krisen. Bd. I. Studier i krisens psykologiske virkninger*. Århus: Aarhus Universitetsforlag.

Petersen, E., Sabroe, K.-E., & Sommerlund, B. (1987) *Danskernes tilværelse under krisen. Bd II. Studier i den plitisk-psykologiske udvikling 1982-86*. Århus: Aarhus Universitetsforlag.

Petersen, Eggert, Andersen, J.G., Dahlberg-Larsen, J., Sabroe, K.-E., & Sommerlund, B. (1989) *De krisebevidste og offervillige danskere*. Aarhus: Psykologisk Institut.

Pittman, D. J. & Snyder, C.R. (Eds.) (1962) *Society, Culture and Drinking Patterns*, New York: Wiley.

Plant, M. (1979) *Drinking Careers*. London: Tavistock.

Politiets Årsberetninger, 1992.

Rasmussen, N. et al. (1988) *Sundhed og sygelighed i Danmark*. København: DIKE.

Rasmussen, O. & Sabroe, K.-E. (1989) *Frequency tables*. Aarhus: Institute of Psychology.

Room, R. (1979) Priorities in Social Science Research on Alcohol. *Journal of Studies of Alcohol*, suppl. 8, 248-265.

Room, R. (1985) Measuring alcohol consumption in the US. Paper ICAA/ ALCOHOL EPIDEMIOLOGY MEETING, Rome.

Sabroe, K.-E. (1984) *Socialpsykologi. Forståelsesrammer og begreber*. København: Akademisk Forlag.

Sabroe, K.-E. (1989a) Alcohol Consumer Consciousness. A social psychological perspective on alcohol. Oslo: National Directorate for the Prevention of alcohol and Drug Problems. *Proceedings 35th. ICAA, Vol. IV, 1-21*.

Sabroe, K.-E. (1989b) Alkoholforbrug og samfundets grupperinger. I Petersen, E., Andersen, J.G., Larsen, J.D., Sabroe, K.-E. & Sommerlund, B. *De krisebevidste og offervillige danskere*. Aarhus: Psykologisk Institut. (også engelsk: Alcohol consumption and the groups of society).

Sabroe, K.-E. (1989c) *Alcohol and Work*. Aarhus: Institute of Psychology, article 5 in this volume, 16 s. (also in Danish).

Sabroe, K.-E. (1990) *Reasons for drinking/not drinking alcohol*. Aarhus: Institute of Psychology, article 6 in this volume, 17 p. (also in Danish in Skrifter fra CANFAU, 1992, *1* (2)).

Sabroe, K.-E. (1991) Alkohol, lav pris, let tilgang - øget forbrug? *Nordisk Alkohol Tidsskrift, 1, no. 2,* april (also in English: Alcohol, low price, availability - increased consumption?, article 7 in this volume)

Sabroe, K.-E. (1991) Ikke ideel forskning, men - ! *Nordisk Alkohol Tidsskrift, 8,* 299-301 (Not ideal research, but - !).

Sabroe, K.-E. (1992a) *Sociale gruppemønstre og alkoholforbrug.* Kapitel til antologi (u. trykn.). (also in English: Social group patterns and alcohol consumption, article 3 in this volume).

Sabroe, K.-E. (1992b) *Storbrugeres sociale gruppeprofil.* Kapitel til antologi (u. trykn.). (also in English: Social group profile of heavy consumers, article 4 in this volume).

Sabroe, K.-E. (1992c) Udviklingen af alkoholforbruget 1988-90. I Petersen, E. et al. *De trivsomme og arbejdsomme danskere.* Aarhus: Aarhus Universitetsforlag. (Development in alcohol consumption 1988-90).

Sabroe, K.-E. (1992d). *Alcohol and drug in the workplace.* Report to ILO/CEC. Geneva: International Labour Office.

Sabroe, K.-E. (1993) *Rusmiddelindsats på regionalt niveau.* Vejle: Vejle Amtskommune. (Substance prevention activities on a regional level)

Sabroe, K.-E. (1993b). Alcohol in Society. In The Amsterdam Group: *Alcoholic beverages and European Society.* Annex I, section 4, 1-48.

Sabroe, K.-E. & Rasmussen, O. (1994) Alkohol Forbruger Bevidsthed. Teori, metode, data. (u. trykn.) (Alcohol Consumer Consciousness. Theory, method, empirical results, in press).

Schiøler, P. (1987) Paper at symposium. University of Erasmus, Rotterdam. Jan. 1987, mimeo, 10 p.

Schutz A. (1971). *Collected Papers.* The Hague: Martinus Nihoff.

Schutz, A. (1974) *The structure of the life world.* London: Heinemann

Sjöberg, L. (1991) Alkoholens risker - upplevda och verkliga. *Nordisk Alkohol Tidsskrift, 8,* 253-267.

Skog, O.J. (1980) Social issues and the distribution of alcohol consumption. *Journal of Drug Issues, 10,* 71-92.

Skog, O.J. (1985) the collectivity of drinking cultures. *British Journal of Addiction, 80,* 83-99.

Sundhedsstyrelsen (1991) *Alkohol- og narkotikamisbruget 1985-89.* København: Sundhedsstyrelsen.

Sundhedsstyrelsen (1991) *Danskernes forbrug af rusmidler.* København: Sundhedsstyrelsen, publik. 15.

Sælan, H. (1984) *Alkohol og alkoholisme. en beskrivelse af en 40-årig dansk befolkningsgruppe.* København: FADL.

Thorsen, T. (1988) Danskerne drikker mere end som så. *Alkohol- og Narkotikadebat, 33*, 16-21.

Thorsen, T. (1990) *Hundrede års alkoholmisbrug*. København: Alkohol- og Narkotikarådet.

Vaillant, G.E. (1983) *The national history of alcoholism*. Cambridge, MA.: Harvard University Press.

Websters Third New International Dictionary 1968.

WHO (1952) Technical Report Series, 48. (Mental Health: 2nd Report of Alcoholism Subcommittee).